The Song Weigher

The Song Weigher

COMPLETE POEMS OF EGILL SKALLAGRÍMSSON
TENTH CENTURY VIKING & SKALD

Translated & Introduced
by Ian Crockatt
with a Preface by Roberta Frank

2017

Published by Arc Publications,
Nanholme Mill, Shaw Wood Road
Todmorden OL14 6DA, UK
www.arcpublications.co.uk

Design by Tony Ward
Printed in Great Britain by
TJ International, Padstow, Cornwall

978 1910345 91 7 (pbk)
978 1910345 92 4 (hbk)
978 1910345 93 1 (ebk)

Cover image and illustrations by Wenna Crockatt

Arc Classics:
New Translations of Great Poets of the Past
Series Editor: Jean Boase-Beier

Contents

Preface

A riddle: What is knotty, coiled, convoluted entangled, bound and fettered, yet still able to move? Answer: the stirring verse of Egill Skallagrímsson, here brilliantly translated by Ian Crockatt. The matter of this verse: battle fury, killing and looting, the shattering of shields, the bloodying of raven's tongue and wolf's gum, grief for friends and things too soon lost. Its makers: wordsmiths skilled in the dialects of invective and flattery, artists who walked the line.

Poets translating poetry often turn to metaphor to illuminate a process dark even to its practitioners: for example, piecing together fragments of a vessel that must match one another in the smallest details, yet need not be like one another (so Walter Benjamin); dancing with a partner, whose rhythms, muscles, limbs, and movements you become familiar with over time (so Craig Williamson). Ian Crockatt speaks of the exoskeleton of skaldic poetry, the crustacean's supporting shell, claws, and body-armour, the bones of the verse for which equivalents must be found in the translator's tool-kit. The skald's metre acts as a grid or net, letting only certain words and clauses through while cleansing them, removing accumulated dross. The sonic factor, the musicality of verse, is at the heart of all poetic translation.

Here, too, Ian Crockatt with his inventive chimes and binding consonants proves himself more than a match for the skald.

Egill's surviving lines in praise of King Aðalsteinn of England are usually accompanied in editions by a prose rendering, a guide to comprehension (however incomplete) but fatal to the poetry as poetry:

> Now the battle-strengthener towering over the land [WARRIOR = Aðalsteinn], chief descendant of kings [KING], has felled three princes; the land comes under the kinsman of Ella [ENGLISH KING = Aðalsteinn]. Aðalsteinn achieved more, everything is lower than the kin-famous royal person; here we [I] swear to this, breaker of the fire of the wave [(lit. 'wave-breaker of fire') GOLD > GENEROUS MAN].
>
> Now the highest reindeer road [MOUNTAIN] lies under bold Aðalsteinn.

Here is Ian Crockatt's rendering in six-syllable lines rich in rhymes and stern and strong alliterations:

Now the stern, tower-strong
strife-intensifier
– king-sired acquirer of
Ella's lands – fells princes.
And he does more. Higher
than high, royal Aðalsteinn –
all've sworn allegiances –
allots wave-cold fire, gold.

Now sheer peaks' deer passes
are paved paths – Aðalsteinn's.

No one not born into a language (in the case of Old Norse-Icelandic this includes all of us) can know how poetry sounded to those for whom it was first composed. Many of Egill's stanzas, taut and reticent, would fit with ease into today's one-hundred-and-forty-character universe, our world of incredibly shrinking messages. Ian Crockatt's translation above not only renders the noise of the original but also captures the meaning behind its sounds. In Egill's praise poem, the English ruler towers over his land, 'higher than high'; he is, as his name ('chief stone') predicts, the top, the Napoleon brandy and Taj Mahal of rulers. Even, asserts the refrain, the "sheer peaks", over which deer pass, have become "paved paths" for Aðalsteinn, the biggest thing on the horizon. The meaning of the royal name is burnished, as in the original, through onomatopoeic tuning.

Egill's beasts of battle are as hungry and bloodstained in Crockatt's translations as in the Old Norse. Here is stanza 11 of Egill's head-ransom poem:

Prose order: Cranes of battle [RAVENS / EAGLES] flew over heaps of the slain; the lips of the wound-mew [RAVENS / EAGLES] were not lacking in blood. Freki (wolf) cut a wound, and point-wave [BLOOD] crashed upon the raven's head-prow [BEAK].

Crockatt's rendition captures both the end-rhymes of the original and Egill's underlying metaphor, which imagines human blood splashing upon the beaks of carrion birds as waves crashing against a ship's prow:

Battle-cranes flew
    where corpse-heaps grew;
blood richly dewed
    red-lipped wound-mews.
Ravening beasts
    tore wounds; blood-yeast
foamed on the prows
    of flesh-beached crows.

The final stanza of Egill's poem in honour of his friend Arinbjörn employs a striking metaphor for poetic creation, that of a landowner ordering a farmhand to perform early-morning tasks in the home-meadow:

Prose order: I was early awake, I bore words together by means of the morning tasks of the speech-servant [TONGUE]. I piled up a praise-pile [POEM] which will stand for a long time uneager to be broken in the home-field of poetry.

Poetic translation:

Up early
    I made my tongue-
smith work; morning's
    first words dawned.
I crafted

this praise-cairn; it
stands high in
poetry's home field.

The poet as builder, as crafter of a monument that will stand high in the field of poetry: Ian Crockatt has accomplished this task with his original, imaginative, and inventive translations. Like many, I used to think skaldic verse was untranslatable. This collection goes some way toward proving me wrong.

Roberta Frank, Yale University

Translator's Introduction

Egill Skallagrímsson was the most original, imaginative and technically brilliant of the Old Norse skalds, those most accomplished of poets whose orally composed and performed verses, packed with flights of fancy in the form of 'kennings' barely contained by the intricate verse forms they used, were as much revered in ninth to thirteenth century Scandinavia as heroism in battle.

Egill was also an impressively bold and cruel Viking, a statement amply backed up by his many self-aggrandising battle and feud poems, expertly composed in the classic skaldic *dróttkvætt* verse form (see Appendix). As an Óðinn-worshipping heathen, who believed in and used the spell-binding potency of runes, formulaic word patterns and symbolic acts such as shape-changing and the magical animation of objects, some of his poems' vitality lies in a quality of pre-christian active participation in living with the earth, sky and sea; not simply on or under them, but as if he were a constituent part of them. At the same time he made poems which demonstrate that he was capable of concern for other people, as well as romantic love. Above all, perhaps, his work highlights the crucial role played in early medieval Scandinavian society by the sustaining support of kinship networks and the benefits and obligations of friendship.

In the poem 'Sonatorrek' (The Terrible Loss of Sons), composed in a more loose-knit form called *kviðuháttr* and able to sustain a lengthy narrative, Egill left us one of the most poignant and bewildered elegies for lost family members we have from any age, as well as it being a lament for the erosion of family-based power, social status and even religious conviction which can ensue. The theme is continued in 'Arinbjarnarkviða' (Arinbǫrn's poem), also in *kviðuháttr* form, a sustained panygeric to a loyal friend to whose diplomacy and courage Egill owed his life. In 'Hǫfuðlausn' (Head-ransom), a heavily ironic praise-poem for his arch enemy Eiríkr Blóðøx and his witch wife Gunnhildr, we have the ultimate coming together of the consequences of Egill and his family's long-term swithering between serving and defying of kings, Arinbjǫrn's unswerving support of Egill, and the power of poetry in this age of war – failure to please the king with the poem would mean he forfeited his head. In fact Egill lived, so the saga tells us, well into his eighties, and during his last years he composed several heartfelt poems about the physical and social humiliations resulting from the loss of his powers in old age.

Egill refers to his pride in himself as a pre-eminent poet, one of Óðinn's chosen 'mead-swillers', as frequently as he refers to his legendary fighting prowess, and together these skills and their deployment form the backbone of one of the most famous of the thirteenth century Icelandic sagas. 'Egill's saga' details his life-story as well as those of his immediate predecessors. He inherited from many of these the physical characteristics he frequently refers to in the poems – massive build, early baldness (*skalla* in his name means 'bald') and exceptional ugliness – as well as his constant opposition to the kings he was supposed to support. The words 'prickly', 'thrawn', 'resentful', 'money-grabbing' and 'vengeful' are apposite in this context; Egill was a notoriously difficult man, and, as many of the poems demonstrate, lethal when crossed.

The mythical origins of Old Norse poetry

Egill's pride in his poetic skills reflects the huge esteem in which the art of making poetry was held, and the magical, shamanistic powers attributed to it stemming, perhaps, from its roots in the mysteries and rituals of the early Scandinavians' worship of a complex pantheon of gods.

The closest we can come to a definition of Old Norse poetry which its composers might recognize was first written down on parchment, using the Latin alphabet, in the thirteenth century. Much of it was composed centuries earlier and orally transmitted from generation to generation. We have evidence that verses were occasionally carved in runes on stone and sticks, and that some of the myths, stories, and adventures of the gods were painted on shields and woven into wall hangings. Amongst the myths that have been transmitted in these various ways before being written down is a tale of the origins of poetry, and a description of the nature of poetry which can be extrapolated from it is *Óðinn's mead.* Many variations on this description are used by Old Norse poets to describe poetry, for example *Kvasir's blood, liquid of the dwarfs, Oðinn's pot-liquid, dwarf's vessel*, but they all refer to the same myth about poetry's origins. To begin to understand the poetry, familiarity with aspects of this myth helps. The following is an abridged version of the thirteenth-century Icelandic scholar and poet Snorri Sturluson's telling of the tale in his *Edda*, and I have based it on the translation by Anthony Faulkes (EDDA, Snorri Sturluson 1987 Everyman pp 61-64).

> Two races of warring gods, the Æsir and the Vanir, agree a truce and spit in a vat to seal the agreement. They create a man, Kvasir, from the spit, gifted with wisdom and the ability to answer any question. Two dwarves kill Kvasir and mix the spit and his blood with honey, then ferment the mix till it becomes a mead which makes a wise man or a poet of any man who drinks it. The giant Suttungr tricks the dwarves – by stranding them on a skerry out at sea – into giving him the mead, which he keeps inside a mountain in three cauldrons, guarded by his daughter Gunnlǫð. Óðinn, initially in the form of a snake, penetrates the

> mountain, then persuades Gunnlǫð to let him have a sip of the mead in return for sex. He sleeps with her on three successive nights, and drains each cauldron of the mead when taking his three earned sips. Then Óðinn transforms into an eagle and flies off with all the mead in his crop. Suttungr pursues him in the form of a hawk. When he gets to Asgard (the gods' compound) Óðinn regurgitates the mead into three containers for the use of the gods, *and those people who are skilled at composing poetry.* He has already defecated a small amount outside Asgard, and that is for poetasters.

Clearly this myth is not intended to be understood as 'real', or as representative of 'truth' or 'fact' as we would understand it now. But what it does indicate is both a way of explaining in narrative and concrete terms what cannot be understood rationally, and the range of experience, emotions, relationships and ideas which are implicitly expressed by it. So poetry might be said to include, or stem from, mythology, gods, war, peace, blood, spit, wisdom, honey, murder, blackmail, sex, deceit, greed, theft, magic, transformation, animals, flight, pursuit, craft, skill, containers, the sea, faeces – a comprehensive mix of real things, bodily experience, practical ideas, and imaginative action. The definition also gives a clear indication of the value placed by early Scandinavian society on poetry – it is god-given, is equated with wisdom, and can only be produced by gods or men who are skilled in the art of making it. More than any other skald's Egill's poetry vividly incorporates the whole gamut of experiences, sensations, thought and feeling the *Oðinn's mead* myth conjures.

Layout, and The Old Norse texts

The early sagas were written in the thirteenth century, most usually by anonymous monks, and their authors drew on orally passed on stories as well as fragmentary older manuscripts which incorporated some of them. The oldest known complete manuscript of *Egill's Saga*, which includes Egill's orally transmitted poems from the tenth century, was written in the middle of the thirteenth century. Of course there are the usual disputes among scholars about exact dating of such old and poorly preserved documents, and indeed about whether all the poems currently attributed to the historical figure known as Egill Skallagrímsson were in fact composed by him. Some have argued that the thirteenth century scribes may have invented some of them, or adapted others, in order to fit with the prose narrative which surrounds them. Others believe the prose saga was written round the pre-existing cannon of Egill's poems and therefore that it was the poems which shaped the saga. It seems certain that the saga only records some of the poems he composed, and there are strong indications that many apparently single poems were taken from lost longer poems.

As it is there are clearly groups of poems amongst

those in the saga which tell a particular story, two obvious ones being those describing Egill's duel with Ljótr the Pale (five poems, pp 76-80), and those recounting the tale of his encounter with Ármóðr the Beard (four poems pp 84-86). Where this is so I have used numbering to indicate the groups. So in the case of the Ljótr the Pale group, for example, the numbering is 30.1-30.5. I have also divided the poems more generally into 'chapters' which link poems very approximately by ages and stages, or themes, in order to assist in giving a narrative context to the individual poems, which already have brief prose introductions to contextualise them. Since they are also arranged chronologically in terms of the saga's time-line, which follows Egill's life-story from the age of three until his old age, I hope the collection overall has a discernible sense of continuity.

The Old Norse texts of the poems, particularly where manuscripts are in poor condition, have been the subject of scholarly scrutiny and debate for centuries. Those used here represent the very latest interpretations by one of the world's foremost Old Norse and early medieval scholars, Professor Margaret Clunies Ross of Sydney University, as prepared for a forthcoming new edition in the Brepols series of editions of the entire corpus of skaldic poetry, entitled *Skaldic Poetry of the Scandinavian Middle Ages*. I am privileged to have been given the opportunity to use Professor Clunies

Ross's pre-publication drafts, and accompanying notes, any or all of which may of course be amended by her prior to their publication as an edition. It is rare for a literary translator of medieval texts to have such a close-up involvement in the developement of new thought about a text by a leading scholar of the day, and I am indebted to Professor Clunies Ross for her generosity, which has given me so much added understanding and focus when grappling with the many difficulties inherent in translating Egill's poems.

About the translations

I have previously referrred to the intricate structure of the skaldic form *dróttkvætt*, which is the form Egill most frequently uses, as 'exoskeletal', akin to a crab's shell, claws and body-armour, and argued that translation which aims to give a genuine flavour of the skaldic originals cannot do so without finding equivalents for their exoskeletal form as well as their highly stylised, hyperbolic language and content. In these translations I have taken the same approach, and this includes the heavily end-rhymed form Egill used in 'Hofuðlausn', unique in Old Norse poetry and possibly echoing Latin and / or Anglo-Saxon verses he could have encountered during previous visits to England.

When it comes to the extraordinary imaginative flights and occasional referential difficulty of the kennings Egill uses – kennings are circumlocutions with metaphorical elements used instead of the nouns they represent (see Appendix) – I have done all I can to reproduce their vivid allusive qualities while also giving a sense of the dictionary meanings of individual words. The Glossary (pp 134-142) unravels some of the more obscure kennings. That said, I work as a translator and poet on the basis that the musical and imaginative qualities of poetry are where the poetry resides, and that skaldic poetry in particular is sold short by efforts to reduce every word and expression that seems obscure to literal sense at first reading. But I do assist, within the poems themselves, by sometimes giving the 'referent' of kennings ie the thing or concept the circumlocutions stands for, as well as the kenning. For example, in the second poem I give the kenning *'ever- / unheard surf-root hounds'* and its referent – 'snails' – in the same line. In addition a note in the glossary helps unravel the kenning – *hounds of the ever-unheard surf-root: surf-root* (seabed), *'ever-unheard'* (silent, to us), *'hounds'* [ironic] = snails.

The one main exception I have made in finding ways to approximate the kennings Egill uses is when the kenning depends for its effect on reference to Old Norse gods, and therefore on the listener/reader having in-depth knowledge of the pantheon of early medieval Scandinavian gods and the myths surrounding them. I have worked on the assumption that most will have come across Óðinn (Odin in anglified form) and be aware that he is an all powerful god of war, though his central role in relation to poetry may be less well known. I have on occasions used attributes of the god in question in my attempts to get close to the original sense – for example using sea images and drinking images when encountering Rán, a sea-goddess who drags the drowning down in her nets, and her husband Ægir, god of the sea and also brewer to the gods – but I am aware that Egill, as a pre-christian Viking with a strong belief in the influence of the gods on human life, loses some of his vitality without the presence of the wide range of gods and myths he refers to.

One way in which I have tried to retain some of the vitality of the Old Norse is by preserving proper names in their original form – so, as above, Óðinn is not changed to Odin for example. I think this also highlights my sense that translation is not simply a matter of replacing one language with another, of making a new version in the new language which feels like a seamless carrying across of idea and image, as though the original's cultural roots need to be subsumed by the culture of the new language. I believe rather that conveying the foreigness of Egill's world is a part of conveying how far from us he is in time and understanding, and yet how relevant he is precisely because these are different, bringing ideas and ways of thinking, and ways of expressing them, that enrich the familiar culture by which we are nurtured but also constrained.

At times the sheer physicality of Egill's poetry, and the breadth of its imaginative reach, have to be matched by the mental effort required of the modern listener / reader to unravel its narrative sense. At other times it is as direct as a slap in the face, and at others it is so inventive that it becomes transformative. By this I mean that a kind of psychic shape-shifting takes place resulting in sensual, intuitive comprehension as opposed to cognitively arrived at understanding. Poems, or parts of poems, conjure or become objects with a presence far beyond the normal scope of language. It's something only the finest poets achieve.

Ian Crockatt

The Song Weigher

Three-Winters Word-Smith

1. Three years old, and left behind when his father and the men of the household are invited to a feast at Yngvar's hall, he follows. He says:

Kommin emk enn til arna
Yngvars, þess's beð lyngva
– hann vask fúss at finna –
fránþvengjar gefr drengjum.
Mun eigi þú, þægir,
þrévetran mér betra,
ljósundinna landa
linns, óðar smið finna.

Youngest amongst Yngvar's
hearth-guests, yes, but worthy,
of the things – heather-thong's
thriving nest-wealth – given
to gilt-tongued men. Giftsman
of the gleam-snake, esteem
my three-winters word-smith's
work; it won't be bettered.

2. While they were drinking that day Egill recited a verse about Yngvar's reward of three snails and an egg for his poem.

Síþǫgla gaf sǫglum
sárgagls þría Agli
hirðimeiðr við hróðri
hagr brimrótar gagra,
ok bekkþiðurs blakka
borðvallar gaf fjorða
kennimeiðr, sás kunni
kǫrbeð, Egil gleðja.

The tough wound-lord – tender
of taloned birds – values
Egill's verse; three ever-
unheard surf-root hounds – snails –
are his reward. World-wise,
the wave-steed rider gave
one more; this moor-duckling's
mattress – its egg – pleased Egill.

3. Aged seven, he brutally murders an older boy who beat him at wrestling. A brawl ensues amongst the adults. His father is angry but his mother takes his side. Egill, imagining himself in the boat his mother thinks should be his reward, says:

Þat maelti mín móðir
at mér skyldi kaupa
fley ok fagrar árar,
fara braut með Víkingum,
standa upp í stafni
stýra dýrum knerri,
halda svá til hafnar,
hǫggva man ok annan.

A swift skiff, my mother
said, should be bought for me,
one beautifully oared,
equipped for Viking trips.
Now I, prow-prominent,
urging my rich-cargoed
war-skiff to safe harbour,
strike one man; another.

Barðr's Farm: Drinking and Magic

4.1. At Barðr's farm they are housed in a barn and given curds because, Barðr says, there is a shortage of ale. Then it emerges that in the main house there is a feast in honour of the *dísir*, female supernatural beings who guard homes and crops, and ale is flowing.

Sǫgðuð sverri flagða
sumbleklu þér (kumbla
því telk brjótr) þars blétuð
(bragðvísan þik), dísir.
Leynduð alls til illa
ókunna þér runna,
illt hafið bragð of brugðit,
Bárøðr, hugar fári.

You tell *me* – Troll-woman's
skull-trouncer – you'll run out
of ale, yet ale is offered
up for spirits to sup.
I call you 'Cairn-spoiler',
'Clever-with-tricks', 'Trickster',
'Hides-strong-hate-from-strangers',
'Seems-straight Bárðr the schemer'.

4.2. Believing his drinking-horn has been poisoned by Barðr, he carves protective runes on it. He reddens them with his blood.

Rístum rún á horni,
rjóðum spjǫll í dreyra,
þau velk orð til eyrna
óðs dýrs viðar róta.
Drekkum veig sem viljum,
vel glýjaðra þýja,
vitum hvé oss of eiri
ǫl, þats Bárðr of signdi.

Carved blood-words serve, crimson
the rune-cut horn, conjure
up beast-rage images –
'auroch's ear-root', 'skull-tree'.
Let's each experience
what eager serving-girls'
ale-brew brings, already
blessed by Barðr's spirit-guests..

Ǫlvar mik, þvít Ǫlvi
ǫl gervir nú fǫlvan;
atgeira lætk ýrar
ýring of grǫn skýra.
Ǫllungis kant illa,
oddskýs, fyr þér nýsa,
rigna getk at regni ,
regnbjóðr, Háars þegna.

I'm dire-drunk while Ǫlvir's
snow-drift pale; we're ailing.
Auroch-spear dregs drizzle
and douse my moustaches.
Spreader of spear-showers
you're spent, can't make a stand
alone. Me, I'm raining
Óðinn-inspired poem-spew.

7. He brags that he evaded capture after killing Barðr by killing some of the men Eiríkr and Gunnhildr sent to find him.

Svá hefk leystsk ór Lista
láðvarðaðar garði
– né fágak dul drjúgan –
dáðmilds ok Gunnhildar,
at þrifreynis þjónar
þrír nakkvarir Hlakkar
til hásalar Heljar
helgengnir fǫr dvelja.

I escaped shrewd Eiríkr's
husbanded acreage in
Listi – I loath boasting –
left Gunnhildr's loamed home-field,
by thwarting three journeymen
– thralls of the valkeries'
tree-hard man – hurried freed
souls to Hel's hall early.

Aðalsteinn and Wolf's-Tooth Reddener

8. He exhorts his brother Þórólfr and their men to attack the town of Lundr before the sun sets on this summer's day.

Upp skulum órum sverðum,
Ulfs tannlituðr, glitra;
eigum dǫ́ð at drýgja
í dalmiskunn fiska;
leiti upp til Lundar
lýða hverr sem bráðast;
gerum þar fyr setr sólar
seið ófagran vigra.

We'll raise, Wolf's-tooth reddener,
our weapons – let sky-high
gleamers fulfil famous
fates in this snake-soothe season.
Let's each reach Lundr quickly,
we'll loose our spell-chanting
spear-torrent there; showers
set off sunset's beauty.

9. Egill responds to an earl's attractive daughter who has made a poem suggesting he has 'not often fed wolves with warm flesh'.

Farit hefk blóðgum brandi,
svát mér benþiðurr fylgði,
ok gjallanda geiri;
gangr vas harðr af víkingum.
Gerðum reiðir róstu,
rann eldr of sjǫt manna,
létum blóðga búka
í borghliðum sœfask.

My sword blade's been bloodied,
my beaked spear's flown shrieking –
stirred wound-birds to stooping;
we strike hard, we Vikings.
Our war-rage made mayhem,
mired rooftops with fire-brands;
blade-lopped corpses littered
lodgings' gore-splashed doorways.

10. Out east they attack Eyvindr 'Vainglorious's' ship. Eyvindr and some of his men leap into the sea and swim ashore to make their escape.

Gerðum hølzti harða
hríð fyr Jótlands síðu;
barðisk vel, sás varði,
Víkingr, Dana ríki,
áðr á sund fyr sandi
snarfengr með lið drengja
austr af unnar hesti
Eyvindr of hljóp skreyja.

We attacked off Jótland's
coast with utmost fury
provoking that bold Viking's –
vaunt-guardian of Denmark –
brave bolt from his wave-horse.
Sand-bound with his war-band
Eyvindr 'vainglorious's'
swift vault and swim saved him.

11.1. Alfgeirr and Goðrekr were earls of Northumbria when king Ólafr of Scotland invaded. King Athalsteinn of England gathered an army and marched north – Egill and his brother Þórólfr fought for him. Egill reports back to his companions about the first phase of the battle of Vínheiðr, in which Alfgeirr ran and Goðrekr died.

Áleifr of kom jǫfri,
ótt víg, á bak flótta,
– þingharðan frák þengil
Þann – er feldi annan.
Glapstígu lét gnóga
Goðrekr á mó troðna;
jǫrð spenr Engla skerðir
Alfgeirs und sik halfa.

Ólafr chased one chieftain,
chose death as the other's
mate in that mire-skirmish;
mighty fighting, I've heard.
But Goðrekr trod wayward
pathways through the sword-swathes;
England's harsh hammerer
holds half Alfgeir's earldom.

11.2. Egill's words over his brother Þórólfr's grave after his death at the battle of Vínheiðr – possibly the same battle as the one known as Brunanburh which took place in 937 in the north of England and is mentioned in the *Anglo-Saxon Chronicles*. Þórólfr had killed an earl named Hringr, and Hringr's brother Aðils killed Þórólfr.

Gekk sás óðisk ekki
jarlmanns bani snarla
(þreklundaðr fell) Þundar
(Þórólfr) í gný stórum.
Jǫrð grœr, en vér verðum,
Vínu nær, of mínum
– helnauð es þat – hylja
harm, ágætum barma.

Courageous, earl-killing,
edge-keenly advancing
through Óðinn's clash-thunder,
Þórólfr the 'thought-strong' fell.
By the broad stream Vina
my brother's mound's growing;
sharp grief for his greatness
grows too, hidden from view.

11.3. Egill brags of his prowess in the battle, having used his famous sword 'Blue Adder' to kill Aðils and many others. He pays tribute to his opponents' military skills. King Ólafr died in the fighting and the Scots and their allies were routed.

Valkǫstum hlóǫk vestan
vang fyr merkinstangir;
ótt vas él, þats sóttak
Aðjils blǫum Naðri.
Háði ungr við Engla
Áleifr þrimu stála;
helt – né hrafnar sultu –
Hringr á vápna þingi.

I piled felled foes' corpses
by the field's west markers.
In that blade-squall's bedlam
Blue Adder slew Aðils.
Ólafr crafted clashes –
sword-clouds ringed the English.
Hringr's troop-throng smithed steel-storms,
staved off ravens hunger.

11.4. Egill sits glowering at the feast after the battle. Aðalsteinn finally proffers the reward of a gold arm-ring on the tip of his sword. Egill accepts it on his sword and, brightening up, is able to respond appropriately.

Hrammtangar lætr hanga
hrynvirgil mér brynju
hóðr á hauki troðnum
heiðis vingameiði.
Rítmeiðis knák reiða
(ræðr gunnvala bræðir)
gelgju seil á galga
geirveðrs (lofi at meira).

Though chain-armoured Aðalsteinn
impales a ringing limb-
hoop – won by my wind-honed
hawk-charmed gibbet-tree arm –
to string on my strong-spined
shield-cleaver, in the spear-
fight he – hawk-fattener –
was far more praiseworthy.

11.5. Aðalsteinn lavishes further gifts on Egill as reward for his battle-prowess and compensation for the loss of his brother. Egill, caricaturing his own grief-stricken face, and ironically praising Aðalsteinn's generosity, says:

Knǫ́ttu hvarms af harmi
hnúpgnípur mér drúpa;
nú fannk þann es ennis
ósléttur þær rétti.
Gramr hefr gerðihǫmrum
grundar upp of hrundit,
(sá's til ýgr), af augum
(armsíma), mér grímu.

My eyelids' brow-mountains
made crags dragged low by sorrow.
One I've found proved able
to ease cliff-face creases.
You, prince, raised these brow-peaks,
found plains in the crags-ground
hoods hide. How fiercely
you hand out loathed arm-bands!

Now, the saga tells us, Egill composed a long poem – a drápa – in praise of Aðalsteinn. Only this stanza and the two line refrain, in which 'sheer peaks' deer-passes' suggest Scotland, survive. The poem identifies Aðalsteinn as an heir of King Ella, an earlier English king.

Aðalsteinndrápa

Nú hefr foldgnárr fellda
– fellr jǫrð und nið Ellu –
hjaldrsnerrandi, harra
hǫfuðbaðmr, þría jǫfra.
Aðalsteinn of vann annat,
allts lægra kynfrægjum,
– hér sverjum þess, hyrjar
hrannbrjótr – konungmanni.

Aðalsteinn's Poem

Now the stern, tower-strong
strife-intensifier
– king-sired acquirer of
Ella's lands – fells princes.
And he does more. Higher
than high, royal Aðalsteinn –
all've sworn allegiances –
allots wave-cold fire; gold.

Nú líggr hæst und hraustum
hreinbraut Aðalsteini.

Now sheer peaks' deer-passes
are paved paths – Aðalsteinn's.

Interlude:
The Lover

16.1. Egill's friend Arinbjǫrn sees him looking depressed, hiding his face in his cloak. Arinbjǫrn thinks he is still grieving for his brother Þórólfr and asks what poetry he has composed recently. Egill responds with this poem. Arinbjǫrn perceives he has hidden the name of a woman he pines for in it – Ásgerðr, Þórólfr's young widow.

Ókynni vensk, ennis
ungr þorðak vel forðum,
hauka klifs, at hefja,
Hlín, þver gnípur mínar.
Verðk í feld, þás foldar
faldr kømr í hug skaldi
berg-Óneris, brúna
brátt miðstalli hváta.

She becomes accustomed
– cliff-walking, hawk-taming –
to age's ugliness;
once brow-peaks soared quickly.
I mask my mocked nostrils'
massive-girthed brow-tower
when her hair's hill-torrent
harries thought with verses.

16.2. Egill protests that he does not hide the names of women in his poems. That said, the woman in question – described as 'stone goddess' and 'walled town of wave-fire' – has seemed less depressed since the warrior-poet drank the intoxicating brew ie. composed poetry.

Sef-Skuldar felk sjaldan
(sorg Hlés vita borgar),
Í niðjerfi Narfa
nafn aurmýils (drafnar),
þvít geir-Rótu gǫtva
gnýþings bragar fingrum
rógs at ræsis veigum
reifendr sumir þreifa.

I'd seldom hide secrets
– stone-goddess's kin-names –
in the giants' intoxicant –
in poetry. It's finished –
the walled-town-of-wave-fire's
widow-grief – since this war-loud
verse-taster's tongue-finger
trawled the god's ale-cauldrons.

Bane of Gunnhildr and Eiríkr Blóðøx

18.1. Egill goes to the Gula Assembly to argue the case before King Eiríkr for his wife Ásgerðr's rights to her father's estates, and the income from them, after her father's death. They had been seized by her sister's husband, Berg-Ǫnundr, who claims Ásgerðr is the illegitimate daughter of a slave. Egill spoke this verse.

Þýborna kveðr þorna
þorn reið áar horna
– sýslir hann of sína
síngirnð Ǫnundr – mína.
Naddhristir, ák nesta
norn til arfs of borna;
þigg, Auða konr, eiða
– eiðsært es þat – greiða.

Thornfoot's boy, Berg-Ǫnundr,
busy being greedy,
asserts my wife – assigning
ale-horn streams – is 'slave-born'.
When I, war's spear-waver,
wed my brooches-goddess
all knew her inheritance.
Hear, kings' sire – I'll swear it.

18.2. Egill loses the case, angering King Eiríkr and Queen Gunnhildr in the process. While escaping their anger he makes this verse about Berg-Ǫnundr.

Erfingi ræðr arfi
arflyndr fyr mér svarfa
– mœtik hans ok heitum
hótun – þyrnifótar;
nærgis simla sorgar
slíkt rǫ́n, ek gek hǫ́num
(vér deildum) fjǫt foldar
(fold væringja) goldit.

Thornfoot's heir has injured
my inheritance chances;
unmannerly name-making
merits 'inheritance-
thief' from me. He threatens,
throws oaths, when I show I've
title to ox-tillings,
would take my snake's-land; gold.

18.3. Egill and his men take to their boats, and are pursued by King Eiríkr's fleet. There is a skirmish during which Egill hurls a spear and kills Ketill, Eiríkr's helmsman. Eiríkr kills ten of Egill's thanes, or free-men, who are guarding Egill's treasure-laden cargo-ship.

Nú hefr þrym-Rǫgnir þegna
þróttharðr, en mik varðak
víti, várrar sveitar
vígelds tíu fellda,
þvít sárlaxa Sýrar
sendr ór minni hendi
digr fló beint meðal bjúgra
bifþorn Ketils rifja.

Ten free-men have fallen,
felled by oak-armed Eiríkr
– his war-flame ran rampant –
but I resist reproach;
my spear – strong-limbed trembler
some skalds call 'wound-salmon' –
flew straight from my fated
fist through Ketill's bowed ribs.

18.4. Egill angrily invokes the gods, seeking their support in condemning Eiríkr for his complicity in the illegal theft of Ásgerðr's estates.

Svá skyldu goð gjalda
– gram reki bǫnd af lǫndum –
– reið sé rǫgn ok Óðinn –
rǫ́n míns féar hónum.
Folkmýgi lát flœja,
Freyr ok Njǫrðr, af jǫrðum,
leiðisk lofða stríði
landǫss, þanns vé grandar.

May high powers punish
proud Eiríkr, make gods' ire
– Óðinn's too – his earnings
for ill-gotten tillage.
Further, may Freyr and Nǫrðr
force the people-oppressor
to give ground. Let land-gods
revile the grave-defiler.

18.5. King Eiríkr eventually declares Egill an outlaw throughout Norway, giving anyone who found him in that country the right to kill him without redress. When Egill hears this he makes another angry poem which mentions that Eiríkr killed two of his own brothers in battle to secure the throne after their father's death, and blames Queen Gunnhildr for influencing Eiríkr against him.

Lǫgbrigðir hefr lagða,
landalfr, fyr mér sjǫlfum,
blekkir brœðra søkkva
brúðfang, vegu langa.
Gunnhildi ák gjalda
– greypts hennar skap – þenna;
ungr gakt ok læ launat,
landrekstr, bili grandat.

Land god, the law-bender
– lust-beguiled – whose sword-thrusts
slew brothers – lays before
me bleak distant vistas.
Gunnhildr, Eiríkr's hound-bride,
I'll have my exile-dues.
Younger, I would avenge
injury instantly.

18.6. While Eiríkr is waging war against his brothers' supporters Egill takes his revenge. He lures Berg-Ǫnundr, his brother Haddr and Eiríkr's foster-son Froði, away from a drinking session and kills them. He recites this poem to his men.

Sǫtum lyngs til lengi
ljósheims bǫrvi þeima
– meir varðak fé forðum –
fjarðǫlna hlut skarðan,
áðr Berg-Ǫnund benjum
bensœfðan létk venjask;
bors niðjar feltk beðju
blóði Hadds ok Fróða.

Over time Berg-Ǫnundr
– I name him 'world-shimmer's
fir-tree', 'fjord's-mackerel',
'fen's-snake' – spent my money;
I was once less easy.
Now I've laid him out – Haddr
and Froði found wounds'-sleep –
in a field's red-cloaked bed.

18.7. After this, Egill's ship attacks a boat captained by King Eiríkr's twelve year old son Rǫgnvaldr, who is going – too late – to warn Berg-Ǫnundr that Egill is in the area. Egill tells his men how he single-handedly killed all the crew, including Rǫgnvaldr.

Bǫrðumk vér, né virðak,
vígleiptr sonar, heiptir,
Blóðøxar rauðk blóði,
bǫðmildr, ok Gunnhildar.
Þar fellu nú þollar
þrettán lagar mána
– stendr af styrjar skyndi
starf – á einum karfa.

We fought – held cheap future
feuds – my blade's bright lightening
gore-grimed with Blóðøxr's
and Gunnhildr's young son's blood.
Thirteen – felled conifers,
moon-gold flecked – died groaning
on one carvelled galley.
I, war-hastener, was the cause.

25. They set sail into an increasing wind. The ship raced along and Egill spoke this verse:

Þél høggr stórt fyr stáli
stafnkvígs á veg jafnan
út með éla meitli
andœrr jǫtunn vandar,
en svalbúinn selju
sverfr eirarvanr þeiri
Gestils ǫlpt með gustum
gandr of stál fyr brandi.

Our gale-blown sea-bullock
– bow honed by hail's chiselling,
stubborn head-winds planing
the spars – 's struck unsparingly;
chilled-steel willow-wolfing
winds mercilessly file
the swan-stem, stream bow-wave
shavings trimmed from timber.

Hǫfuðlausn –
Head Ransom

26. After 2 years on his farm at Borg in south east Iceland Egill grows restless. Deciding to visit Aðalsteinn in England he sets out, but his ship is wrecked in a storm near Grimsby. Realising he has come ashore on King Eiríkr Blóðøx's territory from which he is banished, he goes to York with his friend Arinbjǫrn to face him. He kneels at his feet and says:

Kominn emk á jó Íva
angrbeittan veg langan
ǫldu enskrar foldar
atsitjanda at vitja.
Nú hefr sískelfir sjalfan
snarþátt Haralds áttar
viðr ofrhuga yfrinn
undar bliks of fundinn.

My hard cross-wind canter
– cold that sea-thralled stallion –
seeking the English acres'
strong incumbent was long.
This steely-willed wielder
of wound-flame's gleamings'
brashly sought bold Haraldr's
best kin-strand's sire – Eiríkr .

Gunnhildr, Eiríkr's queen, wants Egill killed then and there in revenge for Egill having killed one of their sons. Arinbjǫrn saves Egill by persuading Eiríkr to spare his life if Egill composes a praise-poem in Eiríkr's honour. Egill is reluctant, but finally agrees, and is given the night to compose the poem. It is known as *Hǫfuðlausn* (head-ransom) and it was sufficiently appreciated by Eiríkr to save Egill's head.

---

1. Vestr komk of ver
en ek Viðris ber
munstrandar mar;
svás mit of far.
Drók eik à flot
við ísa brot;
hlóðk mærðar hlut
míns knarrar skut.

I ventured west.
    Waves in my breast
thronged on Óðinn's
    thought-shore. Ice thinned;
launched when it broke
    my boat of oak
crossed the seaways
    cargoed with praise.

2. Buðumk hilmir lǫð,
þar ák hróðrar kvǫð;
berk Óðin's mjǫð
á Engla bjǫð.
Lofat vísa vann;
víst mærik þann;
hljóðs biðjum hann
þvíat hróðr of fann.

A king's kind ways
  command due praise;
I bring mead-praise
  brewed England's ways.
Praise? Yes I'll sing
  – princes listening –
who, silencing,
  lend praise-songs wings.

3. Hygg, vísi, at
 – vel sómir þat –
hvé ek þylja fet
ef ek þǫgn of get.
Flestr maðr of frá
hvat fylkir vá
en Víðrir sá
hvar valr of lá.

Quiet's the thing;
  hear apt quotes, king;
my well-placed words
  will please – if heard –
men versed in your
  battle-valour;
Óðinn saw gore,
  slain men's pallor.

4. Óx hjǫrva glǫm
við hlífar þrǫm;
guðr óx of gram,
gramr sótti fram.
Þar heyrðisk þǫ́
– þaut mækis ǫ́ –
malmhríðar spǫ́
sú vas mest of lǫ́.

The din of swords
on shield-rims roared;
carnage thickened,
the king quickened
his advance, urging
arm-steel's merging
– blood-surf's surges,
blade-storm's purges –

5. Vasat villr staðar
vefr darraðar
of grams glaðar
geirvangs raðar,
þars í blóði
í brimils móði
vǫllr of þrumði,
und véum glumði.

and tight-warped spears
– too tight to veer,
they met weft-foes
in spear-flashed rows –
brought seal's surf-shores
– thunder-shafts roared –
your blood-wrath's wars
under banners.

6. *Hné folk á fit*
við fleina hnit;
orðstír of gat
Eiríkr at þat.

Shafts felled war-bands
in that wetland;
where steel's clash sounds
Eiríkr's renowned.

7. Fremr munk segja
ef firar þegja;
fró˛gum fleira
til frama þeira:
œstusk undir
við jǫfurs fundi,
brustu brandar
við bláar randar.

Give silence sway,
there's more I'd say,
praise I'd express
for mens' prowess;
wounds gaped when kings'
men were grappling,
bright blades – fresh-steeled –
broke on dark shields.

8. Hlam heinsǫðul
við hjálmrǫðul,
beit bengrefill;
þat vas blóðrefill.
Frák at felli
fyr fetils svelli
Óðin's eiki
í éarnleiki.

Clashed – whet-stone saddlers,
helmet-sun addlers,
wound-engravers –
swords, battle-cravers.
I heard Óðinn's
oak-wood was thinned
when sheaths' ice-rays
slashed in steel-play.

9. *Þar vas eggja at*
Ok odda gnat;
orðstír of gat
Eiríkr at þat.

Eager blades pound,
sword-points resound –
where steel's clash sounds
Eiríkr's renowned.

10. Rauð hilmir hjǫr,
þar vas hrafna gjǫr;
fleinn hitti fjǫr,
flugu dreyrug spjǫr.
Ól flagðs gota
fárbjóðr Skota;
trað nipt Nara
náttverð ara.

King, sword red-stained
by crow-mobbed slain,
when shafts split veins
and gore-spears rained,
you fed, Scots-battler,
myth-wolf fattener
– where Hel corpse-treads –
eagles your dead.

11. Flugu hjaldrs tranar
of hræs lanar;
órut blóðs vanar
benmó ¸s granar;
Sleit und Fleki,
en oddbreki
gnúði hrafni
á hǫfuðstafni.

Battle-cranes flew
where corpse-heaps grew;
blood richly dewed
red-lipped wound-mews.
Ravening beasts
tore wounds; blood-yeast
foamed on the prows
of flesh-beached crows.

12.*Kom gríðar læ*
á Gjalpar skæ
bauð ulfum hræ
Eiríkr of sæ.

There grew wolf-steed's
giant-spurred greed;
Eiríkr's far deeds
made flesh wolf-feed.

13. Beit fleinn floginn,
þá vas friðr loginn;
vas almr dreginn;
því varð ulfr feginn.
Brustu broddar
en bitu oddar,
bǫ́ru hǫrvar
af bogum ǫrvar.

Bows' arrows – loosed –
bit, broke the truce;
when bowed elm sprang,
glad howl-wolves sang.
The vanguard split
when bow-points bit;
flax-strung elm bows
let fly arrows.

14. Verpr broddfleti
af baugseti
hjǫrleiks hvati;
hanns baugskati.
Þróask hér sem hvar
– hugat mælik þar –
frétts austr of mar,
Eiríks of far.

In war's alarms
– king-rich, ring-armed –
casts his speared shield
on sword-play's field.
Heard everywhere –
east-bound ships bear
deeds Eiríkr dared,
truths these words share.

15. *Jǫfurr sveigði ý,*
hrutu unda bý;
bauð ulfum hrœ
Eiríkr of sæ.

The king bent yew –
fierce wound-bees flew;
Eiríkr's far deeds
made flesh wolf-feed.

16. Enn munk vilja
fyr verum skilja
skapleik saka;
skal mærð hvata.
Lætr snót skata
sverð-Frey vaka,
en skers Haka
skíðgarð braka.

I want to add
insights I've had
of his kind ways;
to hasten praise.
Conflict-women
woke the swordsman,
caused ship's shield-strakes
to crack and break.

17. Brýtr bógvita,
bjóðr hrammþvita;
muna hodd-dofa
hringbrjótr lofa.
Mjǫks hǫnum fǫl
haukstrandar mǫl;
glaðar flotna fjǫl
við Fróða mjǫl.

Who gives wrist-gems
– hands out gold's flames –
loathes praise-awards
to locked gold-hoards.
He's hung beach sand-
gold on hawk's-lands;
glad fleets have rolled
in milled grain – gold.

18. Stózk folkhagi
við fjǫrlagi;
gall ýbogi
at eggtogi.
Verpr ábrǫndum
en jǫfurr lǫndum
heldr hornklofi;
hanns næstr lofi.

The common-weal's king
– death-withstanding
when yew-bows twanged
and drawn blades sprang –
throws river-flame;
but land's fist-claimed,
hard-gripped in his;
high praise for this.

19. Jǫfurr hyggi at,
hvé ek yrkja fat;
gótt þykkjumk þat
es ek þǫgn of gat.
Hrœrðak munni
af munnar grunni
Óðins ægi
of jǫru fægi.

Prince, note the ways
my stanzas praise
you. Poetry's food
– silence – felt good.
In my mouth words
– mind-fathomed – stirred
heart-mead's praise-song,
yours; war-wise, strong.

20. Bark þengils lof
á þagnar rof;
kannk mála mjǫt
of manna sjǫt.
Ór hlátra ham
hróðr berk fyr gram;
svá fór þat fram
at flestr of nam.

Prince-praise I brought
 broke peace, prince-wrought;
men found pleasure
 in speech measured.
Praise of war's best
 from laughter's chest
was hardly spurned;
 men heard me, learned.

21. *Njóti bauga*
sem Bragi auga
vagna vára
eðr Vili tára.

Ring-wealth to you!
 May your skalds view
with Óðinn's eye,
 gold-teared wives cry.

27. After he has won the king's mercy by composing and reciting the drápa *Hǫfuðlausn* (head-ransom) he thanks Eiríkr for the present of his head by composing these lines:

Erumka leitt,
þótt ljótr of sé,
hjalma klett
hilmi at þiggja.
Hvars sás gat
af gǫfuglyndum
œðri gjǫf
allvalds syni?

Though my helmet-crag's
  hideous it's
not cheerlessly gained
  from the chief.
Where's the man given
  so fine a gift
by such a high-minded
  king's son as this?

28. Egill and Arinbjǫrn ride south to King Aðalsteinn's court, and are well received. The king asks Egill how he got on with Eiríkr in York. Egill says:

Svartbrúnum lét sjónum
sannsparr Hugins varra
– hugr tjóðum mjǫk mága –
mǫgnuðr Egil fagna.
Arfstóli knák Ála
áttgǫfguðum hattar
fyr regnaðar regni
ráða nú sem áðan.

That hard truth with-holder
– hastener of wave-raven's
blood-feast – allowed Egill
his black-arced eyes. Kin's wise
words won – bold Arinbjǫrn's.
Once downcast, I'm master
of this high-born helmet-
holding crag, as of old.

29. Egill and his party visit a farm called Blindheim on Hod island. It belongs to a young man called Friðgeir whose mother Gyda is Arinbjǫrn's sister. During the first evening Gyda asks Egill whether anything noteworthy happened on their travels. He says:

Urðumk leið en ljóta
landbeiðaðar reiði.
Sígrat gaukr, ef glamma
gamm veit of sik þramma.
Þar nautk enn sem optar
arnstalls sjǫtulbjarnar.
Hnígrat hallr, sás holla
hjalpendr of fǫr gjalpar.

Eiríkr's wrath grew irksome;
I loathed that land-bandit.
Whilst vultures' wings whistle
what songbird can settle?
Arin-bjǫrn helped again –
eagle's lair, hearth-stone; bear.
No life-worn man leaning
on loyal friends falters.

Duel

30.1. A beautiful young woman attracts Egill's sympathy because she is crying all the time. He learns that she is Friðgeir's sister. A man called Ljótr the Pale, who is a berserker and accustomed duellist, has challenged Friðgeir because he and his family have refused Ljótr's petition to marry the girl. Gyda asks Egill to go with Friðgeir, who is young and not an experienced fighter, and Egill agrees on account of his indebtedness to Arinbjǫrn. The duel is to take place the next day on Valdero Island. Egill says to his men:

Esa Friðgeiri fœri,
– fǫrum holms á vit sǫrvar –
– skulum banna mjǫk manni
mey – ørlygi at heyja
við þanns bítr ok blótar
bǫnd élhvǫtuð Gǫndlar
– alfeigum skýtr œgir
augum – skjǫld á baugi.

Young Friðgeir's no fighter;
we'll find this isle of duels,
that ghoul won't be granted
the girl. The wand-whirling
valkerie of spear-storms –
shield-biting inciter,
sick blood-sacrificer –
shoots glares from doom-stare eyes.

30.2. Hearing Egill's words Ljótr challenges him to take Friðgeir's place in the duelling ring. Egill says to his men:

Esat lítillar Ljóti,
leik ek við hal bleikan
við bifteini, bœnar,
brynju, rétt at synja.
Búumk til vigs, en vægðar
vǫn lætka ek hǫnum;
skapa verðum vit skjaldi
skœru, drengr, á Mœri.

Not to allow Ljótr's
little whim might nettle.
I'll play with the pale one's
palsied twig-of-mailcoat
blade – I'm combat-ready.
Be warned, hero, hoping's
hopeless. We'll shape shield's-war
till one lies prone on Moerr.

30.3. Egill prepares to fight Ljótr. He has two swords, one by his side called Naðr (*Adder*) and one in his hand called Dragvandill (*Drawing-wand, Slicer*). While he waits for Ljótr he says:

Hǫggum hjaltvǫnd, skyggfum,
hœfum rǫnd með brandi,
reynum randar mána,
rjóðum sverð í blóði.
Stýfum Ljót af lífi,
leikum sárt við bleikan,
kyrrum kappa errinn
– komi ǫrn á hræ – jǫrnum.

I'll hack with sleek hilt-wands,
I'll hit shields with war-thorns,
I'll hone blades on battle-moons,
I'll blood-redden my swords.
I'll cut off Ljótr's life-line,
I'll lampoon the pale one,
I'll silence boasts with iron –
have eagles ravish his bones.

30.4. When Ljótr enters the duelling ring the fight begins. Egill rains blows on him so furiously that even when backing away to make room to swing his sword he cannot strike back. Ljótr asks for a rest and Egill agrees. He speaks this verse:

Fyrir þykki mér fúra
fleinstøkkvandi nøkkvat
– hreiðisk hodda beiðir
happlauss – fara kappi.
Stendrat fast, sás frestar,
fleindǫggvar stafr, hǫggum;
vábeiða ferr víðan
vǫll fir rotnum skalla.

The fire-brand brandisher
beats a retreat from me;
it seems the hoard-assumer's
afraid of our affray.
The blood-dewed stave-birler
backs off, ducks blade hackings,
flees the field. Bald Egill's
force out-monsters monsters.

30.5. The fight resumes and Egill, overwhelming Ljótr, cuts off his leg below the knee. Ljótr falls and dies. Friðgeir and his men thank Egill, and he says:

Fell, sás flest it illa
– fót hjó skald at Ljóti –
ulfgrennir, hefr unnit;
eir veittak Friðgeiri.
Séka lóns til launa
logbrjótanda í móti,
jafnt vas mér í gný geira
gamanleikr við hal bleikan.

I severed the evil-
achieving wolf-starver's
leg. The poet lopped it,
relieved Friðgeir's grieving.
Don't grant me gratitude,
'lagoon-fire despiser';
out-playing the pallid
one at sword-play was fun.

Poison, Drinking, Runes

35. Egill again brings the case of the lands he believes are rightfully his wife's before the Gulaþing assembly. Atli the Short, Berg-Ónundr's brother, is the defendant. Egill pre-empts Atli's production of twelve witnesses by challenging him to a duel, which is his legal right. Atli accepts, and dies in brutal circumstances. Afterwards Egill, who thinks Atli had put a spell on his sword Dragvandill and that this justified his own actions, says:

Beitat nú, sás brugðum,
blár Dragvandill randir,
af því eggjar deyfði
Atli framm enn skammi.
Neyttak afls við ýti
ǫrmálgastan hjǫrva;
jaxlbróður létk eyða
ek bar sauð með nauðum.

Though drawn, blue Dragvandill
did not bite, would not wound;
Atli's charms had lately
lulled honed blades to dullness.
I hurled hard body-strength
at him, grim incisors
bit the braggart's windpipe.
Bold teeth dealt cold justice.

36. Years have passed. Egill has been living on his farm in Iceland and he and his wife Ásgerðr have had several children. Both Eiríkr Blóðøx and king Aðalsteinn of England are dead. Egill travels to Norway to collect rents from his estates, and visits his old friend Arinbjǫrn. He is warmly received and during one celebratory feast Arinbjǫrn freely gives Egill a magnificent silk gown. Egill says:

Sjálfráði lét slœður
silki drengr of fengit
gollknappaðar greppi;
getk aldri vin betra.
Arinbjǫrn hefr árnat
eirarlaust eða meira
– síð man seggr of fœðask
slíkr – oddvita ríki.

Our choicest man's chosen;
the chief's gift-gown's golden-
clasped silk suits the poet.
Send me a better friend!
Arinbjǫrn's unsparing
acts endow chiefs' powers;
unimaginable,
his equal being born.

37.1. Egill and his men lodge for the night on the farm of Ármóðr 'skegg' (beard). Initially they are offered curds, not beer, and no food. Later copious amounts of strong beer are brought and Egill's men became too drunk to take more. Egill drinks theirs, and Ármóðr ensures many more horns of ale are brought to him. Egill has been warned of potential difficulties with Ármóðr and eventually he gets up, forces Ármóðr against a wall and vomits violently in his face. He says:

Titt erum verð at vátta
– vætti berk at hættak
þung til þessar gǫngu –
þinn kinna lǫ́ minni.
Margr velr gestr, þars gistir,
gjǫld – finnumsk vér sjaldan –
Ármóði liggr œðri
ǫlðra dregg í skeggi.

Evidently I'm eager
to attest to – at best
my trip may prove risky –
your meal; here's cheek-surf gruel.
Let other guests offer
inflated rates for lodgings –
it's rare we meet; Ármóðr,
ale-crud's flooded your beard.

37.2. Ármóðr's men protest and Ármóðr leaves the room, but his wife continues to send a retainer with drink for Egill. Egill drains another auroch's horn and says:

Drekkum ór, þótt Ekkils
eykríðr beri tíðum
horna sund at hendi,
hvert full, bragar Ulli.
Leifik vætr, þótt Laufa
leikstœrir mér fœri
hrosta tjǫrn í horni,
horns, til dags at morni.

Let's drain each drinking-cup,
despite the surf-fighter
dispensing horn-swillings
straight to the hand – this poet's.
I'll not let one droplet
linger, despite him bringing
tarn-swill horns – that stirrer
of sword-play – till day dawns.

37.3. Egill and his men sleep in a barn, and at daybreak Egill re-enters the farmhouse and wakes Ármóðr and his wife and daughter. He draws his sword and grabs Ármóðr by the beard, but Ármóðr's wife and daughter beg for his life. Egill says:

Nýtr illsǫgull ýtir
armlinns konu sinnar
– osss við ógnar hvessi
óttalaust – ok dóttur.
Þeygi muntu við þenna,
þykkjask verðr fyr drykkju
grepp – skulum á veg vappa
vítt – svágǫru hlíta.

The harm-speaking arm-snake
distributor uses
his spouse – I despised
his spear-threats – and daughter.
I'd say you'll consider
this skald's bald exchanges
for tarn's-mash made trash of
trust. We'll fare best far off.

Then he cuts off Ármóðr's beard close to the chin, and gouges out one of his eyes so that it hangs on his cheek, and leaves.

40.1. Egill and his men take breakfast at a farm belonging to a man called Þorfinnr. Þorfinnr's daughter Helga has been suffering from a wasting illness for a long time; not sleeping and sometimes as if 'deprived of her wits'. Egill learns that a local farmer's son carved runes on whalebone and, after they were placed under her pillow, she got worse. Egill burns off the runes and has her sheets aired. He says:

Skalat maðr rúnar rísta
nema ráða vel kunni;
þat verðr mǫrgum manni
es of myrkvan staf villisk.
Sák á telgðu tálkni
tíu launstafi ristna;
þat hefr lauka lindi
langs oftrega fengit.

He's a vain rune-carver
who's unversed in rune-lore;
mis-readings are easy
of old time-dimmed symbols.
I saw ten secret letters
scrim-shawed on whale jawbone;
each twig spelled long illness,
injured your linden-tree.

40.2. Egill carves new runes and Helga's condition improves. Þorfinnr warns Egill that Ármóðr has sent six men to ambush him when he travels on, and offers to accompany him with three of his men. Egill says:

Veizt ef ferk með fjóra
færat sex þás víxli
hlifa hneitiknífum
hjaldrgoðs við mik roðnum.
En ef ek em með átta
esat þeir tolf es skelfi
at samtogi sverða
svartbrúnum mér hjatra.

Know: if I've four fellow-
fighters no shield-wielding
six claims clash of crimsoned
cutters with me. And if
eight stalwart travellers
stride with the dark-browed one
twelve shall not unsettle,
when swords meet, my heart-beat.

Sonatorrek –
The Terrible Loss of his Sons

Egill's son Bǫðvar is drowned at sea, close to the coast and home. Grief-stricken, Egill shuts himself in his room and refuses food and drink. His daughter Þorgerðr tricks him into letting her in, and then persuades him to put his grief into a poem, which she will carve in runes on a stick. Egill composes a poem, now called *Sonatorrek* (The Terrible Loss of his Sons) which refers to other family losses, including another son and Egill's parents.

Sonatorrek

1. Mjǫk erum tregt
tungu ar hrœra
eðr loptvætt
ljóðpundara;
esa nú vænt
um Viðurs þýfi
né hógdrœgt
ór hugar fylgsni.

The Terrible Loss of his Sons

My tongue won't
  – the song-weigher's
sorrow-bound –
  balance breath's sounds.
Can grief-rage
  wrench verse – Oðinn's
mead-haul – from
  my mind's drowned cells?

2. Esa auðþeystr,
þvít ekki veldr
hǫfugligr,
ór hyggju stað
fagnafundr
Friggjar niðja
ár borinn
ór Jǫtunheimum,

Not easy
– anguished – to retch
from thoughts' well
that word-frothed brew;
which Oðinn
once hawked, stealing
– laughter-winged –
from Giantland;

3. .lastalauss
er lifnaði
á Nǫkkvers
nǫkkva 'bragi'.
Jǫtuns hals
undir ðjóta
Náins niðr
fyr naustdurum.

which, pure as
that life-inspired
myth-cargoed
craft, poetry,
spews bloodily
from giants' necks, strands
dwarves' ships at
Hel's boat-shed door.

4. Því't ætt mín
á enda stendr,
sem 'hræbarnar
hlinnar marka';
karskr maðr
sás kǫgla berr
frænda hrers
af fletjum niðr.

For my family
tree is felled;
the culled plane's
a wood-edge corpse.
What man's not
downcast who bears
twig-bones from
his kin's bench-beds?

5. Þó mun ek mitt
ok móður hrer
fǫður fall
first um telja.
Þat berk út
ór orðhofi,
mærðar timbr,
máli laufgat.

First I'll speak
my father's fall;
mother's corpse
carried away:
bear from my mind's
hall green-boughed
talk, leaf-lavished
poem-trees.

6. Grimmt vǫrum hlið,
þats hrǫnn of braut
fǫður míns
á frændgarði.
Veitk ófullt
ok opit standa
sonar skarð,
es mér saer of vann.

A wave cut
    this cruel breach,
broke my father's
    family's ranks;
careless seas
    cancelled my sons,
left this gaping
    wave-gouged gap.

7. Mjǫk hefr Rán
ryskt um mik,
emk ofsnauðr
at ástvinum.
Sleit marr bond
minnar ættar,
snaran þǫ́tt
af sjǫlfum mér.

The sea god
    grapples me down;
frays kin, love,
    fealty, like rope.
Rán's slippery
    seas unknot
kin-love; loss
    unravels me.

8. Veizt, ef sǫk
sverði of rækak
var ǫlsmið
allra tíma;
hroða vágs brœðr
ef vega mættak,
fórk et andvígr
Ægis mani.

9. En ek ekki
eiga þóttumk
sakar afl
við 'sonar' bana,
þvít alþjóð
fyr augum verðr
gamals þegns
gengileysi.

Friends know I'd
    fill revenge-days
with spear and sword,
    drink Swill-smith dry;
crimson bay-
    waves, wind's brothers,
bloody Rán
    that brewer's wife;

but I don't
    think I'd weather
the keel-buckler's
    blows. I'm alone,
un-backed, in
    most men's eyes; an
old lack-friends
    man, bent, futile.

10. Mik hefr marr
miklu ræntan;
grimt er fall
frænda at telja,
síðans minn
á munvega
ættar skjǫldr
afflífi hvarf.

You, sea, have
stolen my best;
recounting felled
kin is hard
since my race's
shield-son strode
down after-life's
sword-arched path.

11. Veitk þat sjálfr,
at í syni mínum
vasa ills þegns
efni vaxit,
ef sá randviðr
røskvask næði
unz Hergauts
hendr of tœki.

I know this;
my son grew un-
corrupted,
composed of stuff
that must have
made a shieldsman
fit, when war-ripe,
for Fate's hands.

12. Æ lét flest
þats faðir mælti,
þótt ǫll þjóð
annat segði,
ok mér upp helt
um verbergi
ok mitt alfl
mest of studdi.

He always
allowed his father’s
words, whatever
the world said;
he upheld me
at home, stood
stave and prop
to my power.

13. Opt kømr mér
mána bjarnar
í byrvind
brœðraleysi;
hyggjumk umb,
es hildr þróask,
nýsumk hins
ok higg at því:

Often moon-bear’s
breath shows me
a brother-less
wind-borne leaf;
I peer round,
as mind-wars rage,
for my half-
glimpsed other; think

14. Hverr mér hugaðr
á hlíð standi
annarr þegn
við óðræði?
Þarfk þess opt
of her gǫrum,
verðk varfleygr
es vinir þverra.

what man's as
mind-strong, will side
with me, halt
hot-headedness?
I need this;
aggressors often
clip our wings
when friends waver.

15. Mjǫk er torfyndr,
sás trúa knegnum
of alþjóð
elgjar gálga,
þvít niflgóðr
niðja steypir
bróður hrer
við baugum selr.

I'll find none
I trust amongst
all under God's
gallows-tree while
truth-blurring
kin-killers take
ring-bribes for
a brother's corpse.

16. Finnk þat oft`
es feár beiðir…
………
………
………
………
………
………

I find those
who demand spoils…
………
………
………
………
………
………

17. Þat er ok mælt,
at engi geti
sonar iðgjǫld
nemar sjálfr ali
enn þann nið,
er ǫðrum sé
borinn maðr
í bróður stað.

And they say
son-gold is not
got unless
fathers beget
new others,
each, in kins' eyes,
born a sub-
stitute brother.

18. Erumka þekkt
þjóða sinni,
þótt sérhverr
sótt of haldi.
Bir es bískips
í bœ kominn,
kvánar sonr
kynnis leita.

Even if
singly I trust
men, I’ve no
pleasure in man.
My wife’s son
seeks his kinsmen
in the half-blind
hung god’s hall.

19. En mér ‘fanst’
í fǫstum þokk
hrosta hilmir
á hendi stendr;
mákak upp
jǫrðu grímu
rýnis reið
réttri halda,

The malt-swill
king’s mindset stands
adamantly
against me.
I daren’t raise
my face-down head,
or ride my mind’s
rune-wise mare,

20. síz son minn
sóttar brími
heiptugligr
ór heimi nam,
þanns ek veit
at varnaði
vamma var
við vámæli.

since fever's
    surf of fire-sword
wounds forced my son
    from this world;
a boy who
    banished disgrace,
guarded his name
    from gossip.

21. Þat mank enn
es upp of hóf
í goðheim
Gauta spjalli
ættar ask,
þanns óx af mér,
ok kynvið
kvánar minnar.

I can't forget
    how Oðinn
lifted our sprig
    to gods-land –
bold ash-tree
    which branched from me,
late bloom of
    my wife's blood-line.

22. Áttak gótt
við geira dróttin,
gørðumk tryggr
at trúa hǫnum,
áðr vinátt
vagna rúni,
sigrhǫfundr,
of sleit við mik.

Life was good:
then the spear-god –
whom I believed,
trusted in;
chose to call Friend,
Chariot-god,
Vanquisher –
quarrelled with me.

23. Blótka ek því
bróður Vílis,
goðjaðar,
at gjarn séak.
Þó hefr Míms vinr
mér of fengnar
bǫlva bœtr,
ef et betr telk.

I'll sacrifice
to him, shield
of gods, but
not eagerly;
yet I judge
the giant's friend
betters me,
makes gain of loss;

24. Gafúmk íþrótt
ulfs of bági
vígi vanr,
vammi firða,
ok þat geð
es gerðak mér
vísa fjándr
at vélǫndum.

The wolf-feeding
war-wager
favoured me
with fault-less skill,
with the wit
to out-word foes –
true conmen,
false connivers.

25. Nú erum torvelt.
Tveggia bága
njǫrfa nipt
á nesi stendr.
Skalk þó glaðr
með góðan vilja
ok óhryggr
Heljar bíða.

But it's tough now:
two-tongue's wolf-
foe's kin stands
stiff on the ness;
she gladdens
me, gives purpose
to this waiting.
Welcome, Hel.

In Praise of Arinbjǫrn

At home in Iceland Egill composes a praise-poem in celebration of Arinbjǫrn, his staunchest friend, and sends it to him on his estates in Norway.

Arinbjarnarkviða

1. Emk hraðkvæðr
hilmi at mæra,
en glapmáll
of gløggvinga,
opinspjallr
of jǫfurs dǫ́ðum,
en þagmælskr
of þjóðlygi.

Poem for Arinbjǫrn

I craft praise
    for kings quickly;
the tight-fisted
    tie my tongue.
I'll champion
    chiefs' deeds in verse,
but not waste
    breath on word-frauds.

2. Skaupi gnœgðr
skrǫkberǫndum,
emk vilkvæðr
of vini mina.
Sótt hefk mǫrg
mildinga sjǫt
með grunlaust
grepps of œði.

Scorn-filled I taunt
tale-tellers,
lavish craft-praise
on comrades;
I've sought lords
– liberal, kind –
with a poet's
openness.

3. Hafðak endr
ynglings burar,
ríks konungs,
reiði fengna.
Drók djarfhǫtt
of døkkva skǫr,
létk hersi
heim of sóttan,

Once I caused
a rightful king's
thunder to rain
threats on me;
I drew down
my daring-hat's
black brim, sought
that bold king's hall

4. þars allvaldr
und ýgshjalmi
ljóðfrǫmuðr
at landi sat.
Stýrðir konungr
við stirðan hug
í Jórvík
úrgum hjǫrvi.

where he sat,
land-rich, terror-
helmeted,
hearing people.
That curb-minded
king in York
held sway with
a blood-soaked sword.

5. Vasa þat tunglskin
tryggt at líta
né ógnlaust
Eirík's bráa,
þás ormfránn
ennimáni
skein allvalds
œgigeislum.

Who braving
Eiríkr's brow-moons
– his dread-gleam eyes –
escapes fear?
Snake-eyes glared
out through the king's
forehead-orbs,
flung terror-light.

6. Þó bólstrverð
of bera þorða
maka hœings
markar drótni,
svát Yggs full
ýranda kom
at hvers manns
hlusta munnum.

But I dared
  deliver them –
salmon-tricked words,
  pillow-talk
smooth – a brew
  that brimmed the cup,
spilled poem-mead
  in all ears' mouths.

7. Né hamfagrt
hǫlðum þótti
skaldfé mitt
at skata húsum,
þás ulfgrátt
við Yggjar miði
hattar staup
at hilmi þák.

King's-men there
  thought my word-swill's
price seemed mis-
  shapen, outsize,
when their lord
  spared this lumpish
hood-filler,
  my wolf-grey head.

8. Við því tók,
en tvau fylgðu,
sǫkk sámleit
síðra brúna,
ok sá muðr,
es mína bar
hǫfuðlausn
fyr hilmis kné,

It's true; and these
two dim stones
sunk deep beneath
sprawled eye-brows,
and this mouth-purse
which poured my
head-fee at
the prince's feet,

9. þars tannfjǫlð
með tunga þák
ok hlertjǫld
hlustum gǫfguð,
en sú gjǫf
golli betri
hróðugs konungs
of heitin vas.

where I took
back many teeth,
with a tongue
and tent-flap ears,
when the glorious
king's head-gift
was thought better
than his gold.

10. Þar stóð mér
mǫrgum betri
hoddfinnǫndum
á hlið aðra
tryggr vinr minn,
sás trúa knáttak,
heiðþróaðr
hverju ráði:

One stood there,
taking my side,
mightier
than most hoardsmen,
a true friend
who earned my faith;
each wise act
increased his worth.

11. Arinbjǫrn,
es oss einn of hóf,
knía fremstr,
frá konungs fjónum,
vin þjóðans,
es vættki ló
í herskás
hilmis garði.

Arinbjǫrn
alone, best of
men, argued
king's-wrath away,
kept friendships
in that chief's court.
Speaking no lies
he saved me.

12. Ok…
…stuðli lét
margrf ǫmuðr
mínna dada,
…
sonar Halfdaner
at í væri
ættar skaði.

Largely illegible stanza. The general sense is that Arinbjorn temporarily defused the feud between Egill and Eiríkr arising from Egill's earlier killing of Eiríkr's son.

13. Munk vinþjófr
verða heitinn
ok váljúgr
at Viðurs fulli,
hróðrs ørverðr
ok heitrofi,
nema þess gagns
gjǫld of vinnak.

They'll call me
    'friend-thief', 'lying
poisoner
    of the poem-horn',
'blame-worthy
    promise-breaker'
if I give
    no tribute for gain.

14. Nús þat sét
hvars setja skal,
bratt stiginn
bragar fótum,
fyr mannfjǫlð,
margra sjónir,
hróðr máttigs
hersa kundar.

All see now
where I site
the incline-
climbing feet of
poetry in
praise of this god-
sired chieftain:
in sight of all.

15. Erum auðskœf
ómunlokri
magar Þóris
mærðar efni,
vinar míns,
þvít valið liggja
tvenn ok þrenn
á tungu mér.

My word-play
when my voice-plane
fashions praise-words
for my friend,
Þorir's son,
can shape double,
triple thought-
sounds on my tongue.

16. Þat tel ek fyrst
es flestr of veit
ok álþjóð
eyru sœkir,
hvé mildgeðr
mǫnnum þótti
bjóðabjǫrn
birkis ótta.

I'll tell first
what all ears hear;
how mild-minded
men find him,
Arin-bjǫrn –
I call "hearth-bear",
"fire-table bear"
"birchs' terror".

17. Þat allsheri
at undri gefsk
hvé hann urþjóð
auði gnœgir,
en Grótbjǫrn
of gœddan hefr
Freyr ok Njǫrðr
at fjárafli.

Everyone
wonders at his
heaping up
of wealth on us;
Freyr and Njǫrðr
have favoured
Hearth-stones bear
with gem-stones' sway.

18. En Hróalds
á hǫfuðbaðmi
auðs iðgnótt
at ǫlnum sifjar,
sem vinreið
af vegum ǫllum
á vindkers
víðum botni.

From his hands,
most famed chief of
Hróaldr's line, flood-
tides of wealth flow.
Kinfolk stream,
friends ride from all
earth's lands scooped from
sky's wind-bowl.

19. Hann drógseil
of eiga gat
sem hildingr
heyrnar spanna,
goðum ávarðr
með gumna fjǫlð,
vinr Véðorms,
veklinga tós.

As a prince's fame
draws in all ears,
his roped us
into hearing.
of all men
most dear to gods,
friend of Vépormr
. . .

20. Þat hann viðr,
es þrjóta mun
flesta menn,
þótt fé eigi.
Kveða skammt
á miðli skata húsa
né auðskept
almanna spjǫr.

Mostly men,
the most wealthy
even, can't match
his conduct.
I can't say
such hearth's aren't scarce;
not all spearheads
house true shafts.

21. Gekk maðr engi
at Arinbjarnar
ór legvers
lǫngum knerri
háði leiddr
né heiptkviðum,
með atgeirs
auðar tuptir.

No-one left
Arinbjǫrn's house –
his longship
of beds – slighted,
no feud-words
followed; his house-
gifts filled weapon-
hands, not war.

22. Hinns fégrimmr,
es í Fjǫrðum býr,
sás of dolgr
Draupnis niðja,
en sǫkunautr
Sónar hvinna,
hringum … ,
hoddvegandi.

He, from his
Fjordane home –
wealth-myths' foe –
wastes Ring-dripper's
golden spawn,
spurns his ring-hoards,
stands against
gold-vat thief-gods.

23. Hann aldrteig
of eiga gat
fjǫlsáinn
friðar spjǫllum.

His fate was
a life-field in
which he reaped
wronged peace's seed.

24. Þats órétt,
ef orpit hefr
á máskeið
mǫrgu gagni,
ramriðin
Rǫkkva stóði,
vellvǫnuðr,
þvís veitti mér.

None would gain
if the gold-hoard-
hater had tossed
life-treasures
on the gulls'-way –
the wave-road
hard-spurred by
our sea-stallions.

25. Vask árvakr,
bark orð saman
með málþjóns
morginverkum.
Hlóðk lofkǫst,
þanns lengi stendr
óbrotgjarn
í bragar túni.

Up early
I made my tongue-
smith work; morning's
first words dawned.
I crafted
this praise-cairn; it
stands high in
poetry's home-field.

Widowed Heels

42. Egill and the poet Einarr 'skálaglamm' (Scales-tinkle) Helgason become friends. Einarr asks Egill when he has been most tested in combat. Egill says:

Bǫrðumk einn við átta
en við ellifu tysar
– svá fingum val vargi –
varðk einn bani þeira.
Skiptumsk hart af heiptum
hlífar skelfiknífum;
létk af ermar aski
eld valbasta kastat.

Once, alone, I fought eight;
I twice trounced eleven,
felled men alone, made warm
man-flesh fresh wolf-fodder.
Each struck with wickedly
wielded swords – shield-shakers.
My tree-sprung arm strongly
spun its unsheathed fire-blade.

43. Egill, an aging man on his farm at Borg in south west Iceland, hears of his staunch and generous friend Arinbjǫrn's death in battle in distant Denmark. He says:

Þverra nú, þeirs þverrðu,
þingbirtingar Ingva,
hvar skalk mildra manna,
mjaðveitar dag, leita,
þeiras hauks fyr handan
háfjǫll digulsnjávi
jarðar gjǫrð við orðum
eyneglða mér heglðu?

Now are trout-bright battlers,
bladesmen who drained silver
horns, diminished; dimness
dawns. Who'll silver hawk's-heights,
shower men with snow-coins,
let snows beyond island-
jewelled, land-looping oceans
land, gleam on poem-trees?

The poet Einnar Helgason visits Egill's home at Borg, but Egill is away. Einarr leaves Egill a magnificent shield, decorated with gold and carved with mythological scenes, in honour of their friendship. At first Egill appears angry because he will have to make a long poem, following the custom regarding such shield-gifts. Then he calms down and says:

Skjaldardrápa

Mál es lofs at lýsa,
ljósgarð, es þák, barða,
– mér kom heim at hendi
hoddsendis boð – enda.
Skuluat at grundar Gylfa
glaums misfengnir taumar
– hlýðið ér til orða –
erðgróins mér verða.

Shield Poem

Time to share the shimmering
ship's top-strake – bright keepsake
given by Borg's gift-rich
guest-poet – in dróttkvætt.
I'll harness the sea-horse
– harbour mead-dwarves word-hoard –
with a tight rein, entertain
ears tuned to skald-speak. Hear!

The rest of the poem is lost.

44. Egill's son Þorsteinn wears Egill's splendid cloak, a treasured gift from Arinbjǫrn, to the annual assembly. Afterwards he returns it to the chest it came from, muddied, without telling Egill. His mother Ásgerðr is aware of the incident. Much later Egill discovers the cloak is muddy and questions Ásgerðr until she tells him what happened. Egill says:

Áttkak erfinytja,
arfa mér til þarfan;
mik hefr sonr of svikvinn
– svik telk í því – kvikvan.
Vel mætti þess vatna
viggríðandi bíða
es hafskíða hlœði
hljótendr of mik grjóti.

He's brought no benefits,
my beneficiary.
My heir-son's kin-crooked,
connives while I'm alive.
The water-steed steerer's
mistaken, taking
what's mine. Won't wave-bravers
wait till boulders shroud me?

A ship arrived one morning, and its helmsman, Þormóðr, brought Egill a shield sent to him by Egill's son Þorsteins. Egill composed a shield-drápa in its honour, and this is the first verse, the only one we have. Egill says:

Heyri furs á forsa
fallhadds vinar stalla,
hyggi, þegn, til þagnar
þínn lýðr, konungs, mína.
Oft skal arnar kjafta
ǫrð góð of trǫð Hǫrða,
hrafnstýrandi hræra
hregna, mín of fregnask.

Hear, king's thane, how water's
hewn to good verse – the thrawn
god's altar-fire's flowing –
should friends hear to the end.
Good, sea-raven's steersman,
when seed-surf of eagles –
poetry – pours into
Hordalanders' ear-porches.

45. Egill and various family members have adjoining farms near Borg. Disputes with a difficult neighbour, Steinarr Ǫnundarson, are poorly handled by his nephew, Þorgeirr Blundr, nicknamed 'Dozy'. Egill discusses the situation with his son Þorsteinn, recalling how he gained the disputed land from Steinarr.

Spanðak jǫrð með orðum
endr Steinari ór hendi;
ek þóttumk þá orka
arfa Geirs til þarfar.
Mér brásk minnar systur
mǫgr, hétumk þá fǫgru;
máttit bǫls of bindask
Blundr; ek slíkt of undrumk.

My words turned sound-weapons,
won land from Steinarr's hands;
I thought I'd got grazing
for Geirr's inheritor –
my sister's son. Promise
stays unfulfilled; failure's
dogged Dozy. Amazing,
his dealings with evil.

46.1. Some women laugh at Egill when, in his old age, he trips and falls. His step-daughter's husband Grímr remarks that women don't value men once they are old. Egill says:

Vals hefk vǫfur helsis,
váfallr em ek skalla,
blautr erum bergifótar
borr, en hlust es þorrin.

Skull cants in its collar.
Could pitch on my bald-patch.
Thighs' bore-tongue stays spongy.
Sound starves in my ear-caves.

46.2. Blind and unsteady on his feet, Egill gets in the way of a woman cleaning the room when he tries to get warm by the fire. She tells him to go to bed and let her get her work done.

Hvarfak blindr of branda,
biðk eirar Syn geira;
þann berk harm á hvarma
hnitvǫllum mér, sitja,
enn jarðgǫfugr orðum
(orð mín) konungr forðum
(hafði gramr at gamni)
Geirhamðis mik framði.

I – who blindly blunder
behind hurt-pride eyelids,
who seek peace from skirt-girls
to sit beside firesides –
once stood – choice of chieftains –
chanting trenchant refrains.
Great-kingdomed kings of old
coined me giants'-words – gold.

46.3. Egill goes close to the fire to warm his feet, and a man warns him not to go too close. Egill's two wives are long dead. He says:

Langt þykki mér,
 ligg einn saman,
Karl afgamall
 á konungs vǫrnum;
eigum ekkjur
 allkaldar tvær,
en þær konur
 þurfu blossa.

Days are prolonged.
 I lie alone.
decrepit, old –
 a king uncrowned.
My widowed heels
 hug in the cold –
two chilled women
 wanting life's warmth.

Appendix: Verse Form and Kennings

VERSE-FORM

Skaldic poetry is notorious for the complexity of its verse-form which, since it was composed orally, was defined entirely by its sound patterns and rhythms. The form in which we write it down now reflects these, but in the Icelandic sagas poetry was written down like prose and is often visually indistinguishable from the text round it. This may reflect the high cost of vellum in early medieval Iceland.

Each classic skaldic stanza, known as *dróttkvætt,* which means 'verse suitable for reciting before the court', is composed of a system of eight six syllable lines with pre-set patterns of stress, alliteration, internal full-rhyme and half-rhyme and trochaic line-endings. The majority of Egill's stanzas are composed in this strict form. An example is given below, with the alliteration and internal rhyme and half-rhyme schemes indicated by bold letters and underlining respectively. The approximations of the translated poem are evident.

Sǫgðuð **s**verri flagða	You **t**ell *me* – **T**roll-woman's
sumbleklu þér (kumbla	skull-**t**rouncer – you'll run out
því telk **b**rjótr) þars **b**létuð	of **a**le, yet ale is **o**ffered
(**b**ragðvísan þik) dísir.	**u**p for spirits to sup.
Leynduð **a**lls til **i**lla	I **c**all you '**C**airn-spoiler',
ókunna þér runna	'**C**lever-with-tricks', 'Trickster',
illt hafið **b**ragð of **b**rugðit,	'Hides-**str**ong-hate-from-**str**angers',
Bárøðr, hugar fári.	'Seems-**str**aight Bárðr the schemer'.

Briefly, it should be noted that each stanza's eight lines is made up of two sets of four – a few of the poems are only four lines long – and each six syllable line ends with a trochee, that is a stressed syllable followed by an unstressed syllable. The last syllable is generally unrhymed, and the internal half-rhymes and rhymes are on syllables, not necessarily whole words. Full rhymes occur in even lines, half-rhymes in odd lines. The alliterative pattern, which ties the lines together in twos, means odd lines have two alliterating syllables, and the first stressed syllable of the following even line alliterates with them. So in the Old Norse poem above the '*s*'s of *Sǫgðuð* and *sverri* in line one alliterate with the '*s*' of *sumbleklu* in line two, and in the translation the '*t'* s of *tell* and *troll* alliterate with the 't' of *trouncer* in its line two. These basic rules are complicated by unpredictable word order which means it is not always obvious which word relates to which unless the reader has a full grasp of Old Norse grammar. A further complication is the skalds' frequent use of 'intercalation', a technique in which a sentence is interrupted by a phrase, or another sentence, and then continued, the effect being to both slow down the rhythm and to insert more information in the building up of a picture or situation. An example in the above translation is Egill's threatening description of himself as *troll-woman's / skull trouncer* which interrupts the sentence *'you tell* me... *you'll run out of ale'*.

Egill uses the looser form called *Kviðuháttr* for his longer poems, which is a variant of the form *Fornyrðislag*, a verse pattern found in the literatures of many Germanic-based languages, including Anglo-Saxon. *Kviðuháttr* generally consists of an eight line stanza, in which lines 1,3,5 and 7 have three syllables, and lines 2,4,6 and 8 have four. Each pair of lines alliterates on a minimum of one stressed syllable in the three syllable line with, ideally, the first stressed syllable in the four syllable line. The following example is from *Sonnatorek*

Esa auðþeystr,	Not **e**asy
þvít **e**kki veldr	– **a**nguished – to retch
hǫfugligr,	from thoughts' **w**el
ór **h**yggju stað	that **w**ord-frothed brew;
fagnafundr	which **O**ðinn
Friggjar niðja	**o**nce hawked, stealing
ár borinn	– **l**aughter-winged –
ór Jǫtunheimum,	from Giant-**l**and

It is not always easy to stick closely to the aim of having the alliteration in the four syllable lines confined to the first stressed syllable – the last line above is an example. There are many examples also where I have reversed the line pattern so that the four stressed line comes first, simply because it made it more possible for me to make the poetry work.

The other main form that Egill uses is called *Runhent,* and this is confined to *Hǫfuðlausn,* the 'head-ransom' poem Egill composed in carefully exaggerated praise of his enemy Eiríkr Blóðøx. *Runhent* is almost unique in extant Old Norse literature, the only other examples we have of it being two short poems by Egill's father. It features full end-rhymes, usually in short couplets, but sometimes for up to four consecutive lines. Most stanzas have eight lines, a few have four. All the lines have four syllables, and the alliteration pattern is the same as that described above for *Kviðuháttr*.

Hygg, **v**ísi, at	**Q**uiet's the thing;
– **v**el sómir þat –	hear apt **q**uotes, king;
hvé ek **þ**ylja fet	my **w**ell-placed words
ef ek **þ**ǫgn of get.	**w**ill please – if heard –
Flestr maðr of frá	men **v**ersed in your
hvat **f**ylkir vá	battle-**v**alour;
en **V**íðrir sá	Óðinn **s**aw gore,
hvar **v**alr of lá.	**s**lain men's pallor.

Once again the translation falls short of the ideal – in lines 4 and 7 for example, the alliteration falls on an unstressed syllable instead of a stressed syllable. The tightrope walked between formal accuracy – so crucial to the skalds – and capturing the vigour and skill of the poetry tends to wobble from time to time.

Kennings

Kenning is an Old Norse word but kennings were not exclusively used by Scandinavian skalds. It is a form of speech characteristic of the literatures of many Germanic-rooted languages, including

Anglo-Saxon. The *Beowulf* poet used them, for example referring to a ship's sail as *mere-hrægl* (sea-garment) which wraps itself round the mast, and the sea as *swan-rād* (swan's road, or riding place). These convey the method and impact of kennings, the way they tie two objects together in a way that gives a vivid filmic quality to a third, the object they replace. We have modern examples too, circumlocutions which follow the pattern of one noun or phrase linked to another in the genitive case to make a picture suggesting a third – 'sky-scraper' (scraper of the sky = tall building), cannon-fodder (food of cannon = infantry) for example.

Egill was a master at creating kennings which stretch the alertness and imaginative powers of his audiences, and at re-imagining and extending kennings which were already part of the skaldic tradition. Many kennings reference ancient Scandinavian mythology and stories of their gods which adds further complications for the reader unaccustomed to them. The kennings are woven into the fabric of the poem, and the images they conjure are often supported by other words and expressions in it. Egill's very first poem, allegedly composed when he was three years old, has several kennings, and associated references and inferences. My translation goes as follows:

Youngest amongst Yngvar's
hearth-guests, yes, but worthy
of the things – heather-thong's
thriving nest-wealth – given
to gilt-tongued men. Giftsman
of the gleam-snake, esteem
my three-winters word-smith's
work; it won't be bettered.

heather-thong's thriving nest-wealth –' heather-thong' (thong of heather) = snake. A snakes's *nest-wealth* (wealth of the snake's nest) = gold, since treasure hoards were, in myth, guarded by dragons / snakes

giftsman of the gleam-snake – 'gleam-snake' refers again to gold, often given in the form of a golden ring or armband, and a man who give gifts of gold is the king or lord the skald and warriors serve and are rewarded by. The best lords are the most generous 'giftsmen'.

gilt-tongued men = 'Gilt-tongued men' are poets, who both speak golden words and are rewarded for them with gold.

word-smith – 'word-smith' (smith of words) is a poet, one who forges poems in the mind's fire as the blacksmith forges swords in the smithy.

Egill's plea to be rewarded for his work with 'things... that are given to gilt-tongued men' is given authority by the skill with which his use of kennings reminds the lord (Yngvar) that he is a giftsman who rewards poets with gold, that he, three year old

Egill, knows the traditions underlying the kennings, and his confident use of them is evidence that he is a skilled poet.

For many simple words – or 'referents' as they are known in the context of kennings – there are scores of mostly unique kennings in the corpus of skaldic poetry, with kennings for 'sword/s' (388), 'battle' (647), and 'warrior/s' (949) being pre-eminent. Some of Egill's kennings for these referents, sometimes adapted in translation, include:

> Battle: *Óðinn's clash-thunder, blade-storm, blade-squall, mire-skirmish, arm-steel's merging, steel-play etc*
> Warrior: *wolf's-tooth reddener, hawk-fattener, war-hastener, strife-intensifier, spreader of spear-storms, wielder of wound-flame's gleamings, Troll-woman's skull-trouncer*
> Sword: *wound-engraver, wound-flame, war-flame, sheath's ice-ray*
> Birds of prey: *red-lipped wound-mews, battle-crane,*
> Ship: *wave-steed, sea-thralled stallion*

These, along with many others, are explained in the glossary which follows.

Glossary

Poem 1 – *heather-thong's* (snake's*) thriving nest-wealth* (gold): treasure, traditionally guarded by a snake
giftsman (lord, giver of rewards) *of the gleam-snake* (gold): Yngvar

Poem 2 – *wound-lord*: warrior chieftain
ever-unheard (silent, to us) *surf-root* (seabed) *hounds* [ironic]: snails.
wave-steed (boat) *rider*: seafarer

Poem 4.2 – *auroch's* (wild beast's) *ear-root* (part of the skull): drinking horn

Poem 4.3 – *auroch* (wild beast*)-spear* (horn) *dregs* (swill): mead swill
spreader of spear-showers: warrior
raining Óðinn-inspired poem-spew: vomiting (god-given) poetry

Poem 7 – *Valkeries* (warrior goddesses who chose which men would die in battle) *tree-hard man* (tough warrior): instrument of the Valkeries
*Hel's (*Goddess presiding over the world of the dead) *hall*: Hell

Poem 8 – *Wolf's-tooth reddener*: one who leaves slain enemies as carrion for wolves to eat; warrior
sky-high gleamers: swords held up
snake-soothe season: the season snakes enjoy most; summer

Poem 9 – *stirred wound-birds* (birds of prey) *to stooping:* created carrion for birds to swoop down onto and eat; killed men in battle.

Poem 11.2 – *Óðinn's clash-thunder:* battle

Poem 11.3 – *blade-squall:* battle
steel storm: battle
staved off ravens' hunger: fed ravens carrion; killed men

POEM 11.4 – *ringing-limb-hoop:* golden arm-ring
wind-honed/hawk-charmed gibbet-tree arm: a difficult set of readings in a garbled Old Norse manuscript. The kennings combining tree, gibbet and arm images suggest that Egill's arm carries death – in the form of the hawk that kills and also eats bodies of men Egill has killed, as well as it being his sword-arm – and that in that sense it is therefore a gallows in itself, or kin to a gallows-tree. So the reward of the arm-ring given by Aðalsteinn is for Egill's lethal performance on the battlefield.
shield-cleaver: sword

POEM 11.5 – *brow-mountains*: eyebrows
plains in the crags-ground: pleasant features in the harsh landscape (of his face)
How fiercely you farm out loathed arm-rings!: Aðalsteinn rewards his retainers so generously it seems he hates gold; a standard piece of praise-poem hyperbole.

POEM AÐALSTEINNDRÁPA – *drápa*: poem sequence with refrain; so, drápa about Aðalsteinn
wave-cold (cool, glistening) *fire:* gold

POEM 16.1 – *brow-peaks:* eyebrows
massive-girthed brow-tower: huge nose. The phrase, contrary to Egill's protest in poem 16.2, includes a concealed reference to Ásgerðr's name – mASsive-GIRTHed
[In the old Norse, the method of concealment is much more complex. The following is Margaret Clunies Ross's note to her as yet unpublished new edition of the Old Norse texts of Egill's poetry:

> poets had to take great care to conceal the names of the objects of their affection, hence the frequent use of the rhetorical device of *ofljóst*, lit. 'excessively clear' in poetry of this kind, as in ll. 5-8 of this stanza. *Ofljóst*

depends on punning word-play, in which a homonym of a noun which forms part of a kenning or is a kenning-referent (and which also forms the whole or a part of the name of the beloved) must be substituted for the given term in order to discover the concealed name. Here the name consists of two elements, *Ás-gerðr*, so the poet composes a complex kenning in which both elements are concealed in homonyms. In the kenning *faldr foldar berg-Óneris, faldr* 'woman's headdress', is more or less synonymous with *gerða* 'snood, article of woman's clothing' (cf. LP: gerða 1), while the first element of Ásgerðr's name is concealed in the referent of the kenning *fold berg-Óneris*, 'earth of rock-Ónerir' [GIANT > MOUNTAIN]. The 'earth' of a giant is a mountain, as giants typically inhabit such places, according to ON myth; one meaning of the noun *áss* is 'rocky ridge', and this must then be substituted for the more general sense of the kenning referent to give the first element of Ásgerðr's name.]

POEM 16.2 – This stanza, and particularly lines 5-8, is also extremely difficult to unravel.

stone-goddess: probably alludes to precious stones, so complimenting Ásgerðr whom Egill is again secretly referring to in the poem – while denying that that he would normally do that.

Lines 5-8 consist of three highly complex kennings, involving several substitutes for Ásgerðr's name, and I cannot claim to have got near the detailed sense of them in my translation.
the-walled-town-of-wave-fire: possibly a kenning for the gold-enriched woman he protects by not naming her in the poem
widow-grief: Ásgerðr was Egill's brother Þórólf's wife, and it is not long since Þórólf was killed in battle (see poem 11.2)

trawling the god's ale-cauldrons: fishing for inspired words to make the poem
The overall sense of the stanza, as it seems to me, is that Egill pretends he would not refer to a lady he desires in a poem, but repeatedly does so by disguising her identity in the complexities of his allusive verse, and that she seems to be more cheerful since he has done so.

POEM 18.1 – *assigning ale-horn-streams:* organizing the serving of ale to guests, the role of the lady of the house
war's spear-waver: warrior
brooches-goddess: his jewelled bride (Ásgerðr)

POEM 18.3 – *war-flame:* sword

POEM 18.6 – *world-shimmer's fir-tree:* tree of the bright world; man
fjord's mackerel: fish, water-snake; gold;
fen's snake: gold;
overall meaning of the combined kennings = wealthy man, in this case Berg-Qnundr
wounds'-sleep: death

POEM 18.7 – *felled conifers, moon-gold flecked:* trees of gold; men

POEM 25 – *sea-bullock:* ship

POEM 26 – *sea-thralled stallion:* ship
wound-flames gleamings: bright swords

POEM HQFUÐLAUSN: HEAD RANSOM
HFL 1 *waves in my breast thronged on Óðinn's thought-shore*: poetry
HFL 2 *brewed England's way:* reference to the use of end-rhymes in this poem, almost uniquely in Old Norse poetry, thought to have been adopted by Egill after encountering the form in Anglo-Saxon and/or Latin poems on previous visits to England.

HFL 4 *blade-storms*: battle
HFL 5 *seals' surf-shores:* the sea
HFL 8 *whet-stone saddlers:* swords; their horse-rider-like movement to and fro on the whet-stone – the blade 'saddles' it – when being sharpened
helmet-sun addlers: swords; clashing on bright helmets, confusing the helmet wearer
wound-engraver: swords
Óðinn's oak-wood: wood of men; army
sheath's ice-rays: swords
steel-play: battle
HFL 10 *myth-wolf fattener...where Hel corpse-treads:* refers to Fenrir, mythical wolf, who's sister Hel ruled the world of the dead, and the convention of warriors 'feeding eagles' with the bodies of the slain.
HFL 11 *battle-cranes:* eagles
Wound-mews: birds of prey
HFL 15 *wound-bees:* arrows
HFL 16 *conflict-women:* Valkeries; war goddesses, choosers of the slain
HFL 17 *wrist-gems...gold's flames:* golden bracelets
he's hung beach-sand gold: hung gold bracelets *on hawk's-lands:* arms
glad fleets: seafarers *have rolled in milled grain*: grain milled in Fróði's mill, which in legend milled golden flour
river-flame: sea-bound sword-play ie renowned for his fighting far and wide
land's fist-claimed: land taken by force ie his lands in England
HFL 20 *laughter's chest:* the breast. He may be mocking Eiríkr at this point.
HFL 21 *view with Óðinn's eye:* the eye of wisdom and fore-telling

gold-teared wives cry: a reference to the Goddess Freyja who wept tears of red gold when her husband was away from home.

POEM 27 – *helmet-crag:* head
wave-raven's blood-feast: war; battle

POEM 29 – Arin-bjǫrn's two part name is hidden in the phrase *arnstalls sjǫtulbjarnar* in line six of the Old Norse stanza. His name translates as I have shown in my line six.

POEM 30.3 – *hilt-wands:* swords; *war-thorns:* swords
battle-moons: shields

POEM 30.4 – *fire-brand brandisher:* sword-brandisher; warrior
stave-birler: stave-twirler; warrior

POEM 30.5 – *Wolf-starver:* one who fails to feed wolves ie kill men for wolves to eat; beaten warrior
Lagoon-fire gold *despiser:* one who hates gold, does not ask reward

POEM 37.1 – *cheek-surf gruel:* vomit

POEM 37.2 –*surf-fighter:* seafarer
horn-swillings: ale in horns; *tarn-swill horns*: horns of ale
stirrer of sword-play: inciter to fight

POEM 37.3 – *arm-snake distributor:* lord, giver of gold arm-rings; in this case Ármóðr
tarn's-mash: ale

POEM 40.1 – *linden-tree:* woman, in this case their daughter Helga. (The full kenning is *linden-tree of leeks*)

POEM 40.2 – *clash of crimsoned cutters* (sword-blades): battle
the dark-browed one: Egill

SONATORREK: THE TERRIBLE LOSS OF SONS

SK 2 *word-frothed brew* (poetry) and *Óðinn once hawked..... from Giantland* are references to the myth of Óðinn's acquisition of the fermented brew which is the source of poetry – see Introduction

Sk 3 *spews bloodily...boat shed door...*while the sense is unclear, there may be reference to the myth in which Óðinn and his brothers behead a giant and his blood becomes the sea, as well as further reference to the origins of poetry myth, the part in which dwarves are stranded in a boat by the giant Suttungr on a skerry, forcing them to reveal where he has hidden the mead of poetry.

Sk 7 *Rán:* sea goddess who receives the drowned.

Sk 8 *swill-smith:* maker of ale; the sea-god Ægir, who is also the brewer to the gods; *crimson:* used here as a verb.

Sk 9 *keel-buckler:* the sea

Sk 10 *my race's shield-son:* my son, protector of the family

Sk 12 *stave and prop:* poetical terms referring to alliterative and stress patterns which hold poems together, and here underlining the theme of the loss of his sons' role in maintaining his own, and therefore his family's, status and safety.

Sk 13 *moon-bear's breath...wind-borne leaf:* he often thinks (*moon bear* is a giant and wind of a giant is 'thought') of his dead brother – Þórólf (see poems 8 and 11.2) – looks out for him in battle and feels adrift, like a leaf on the wind, without him.

Sk 15 *god's gallows-tree:* the world

Sk 16 The manuscript is too damaged to read

Sk 17 *son-gold*: compensation paid in certain situations for the loss of a son

Sk 18 *half-blind hung god:* Óðinn, who having sacrificed an eye to receive wisdom by drinking from the well of Mimir, hung for nine nights from the great ash tree Yggdrasill – world-gallows, tree of life – to gain more.

Sk 19 *malt-swill king*: Ægir, god of the sea and brewer to the gods.

Sk 20 *fever's surf of fire-sword wounds*: battle image describing the heat and pain of the fever that killed one of his sons
Sk 23 *shield of gods:* Óðinn, leader of the gods; *Giant's friend*: Óðinn
Sk 24 *wolf-feeding war-wager*: Óðinn, god of war
Sk 25 *Two-tongue's wolf-foes kin stands*: Hel, overseer of the world of the dead, waiting to claim Egill. Her brother is Fenrir, the giant wolf whose escape from the chains in which the gods restrained him is part of the final horror of Ragnorok, the end of the world, during which Fenrir devours Óðinn.

Arinbjarnarviða: Arinbjǫrn's Poem

Ar 5 *brow-moons... forehead-orbs:* eyes
Ar 6 *salmon-tricked words, pillow-talk smooth:* snake-clever words, smooth as those Óðinn talked when he bedded Gunlóð in order to steal the mead of poetry (see Introduction).
a brew that brimmed the cup: the poem he made
Ar 7 *word-swill's price:* the reward for his poetry – his head (see *Hǫfuðlausn*, p. 61)
Ar 17 *Freyr: a* fertility god, *Njǫrðr:* Freyr's father, associated with wind and sea.
Hearth-stones bear: Arinbjǫrn
gem-stones sway: riches
Ar 18 *Sky's windbowl:* heaven
Ar 19 *Véparmr:* an unknown god
Ar 22 *wastes Ring-dripper's golden spawn:* discards the Draupnir's (a race) gold rings. The last four lines of this stanza all emphasise Arinbjórn's disdain of riches, ie his generosity in giving them to others.
Ar 24 *gull's way...the wave-road:* the sea
sea-stallion: ship
Ar 25 *this praise-cairn:* this poem

POEM 42 – *tree-sprung :* strong, flexible
unsheathed fire-blade: sword

POEM 43 – *trout-bright battlers:* gleaming warriors
who'll silver (used here as a verb *)hawk's heights* (arms, hands): reward me with money
shower me with snow-coins: as above
snow... let gleam on poem-trees?: money (given by distant lords) to poets – ie now Arinbjǫrn has gone, the age of generous lords who richly rewarded poets has gone too.

SKALDJARDRÁPA: SHIELD POEM
ship's top-strake: shields, which were fastened to the top plank of warships' sides
dróttkvætt: poem fit to be recited at court
harness the sea-horse...with a tight rein: 'rig the ship carefully', but also *dwarves-ship* is poetry, so in this context 'shape the poem rigorously'

POEM 44 – *water-steed (*ship) *steerer:* ship's helmsman
wave-bravers: seafarers

BERUDRÁPA: SHIELD POEM
water's hewn to good verse...the thrawn god's alter-fire's flowing: Óðinn is known as the 'friend of alter-fire', and 'Óðinn's waterfall' is poetry.
Sea-raven's steersman: ship's helmsman

POEM 46.1 – *thighs' bore-tongue:* penis

Biographical Note

Ian Crockatt's poetry has won many prizes and commendations in national and international competitions. His books include *Flood Alert* (Chapman Publishing, 1996); *The Crucifixion Bird* (Northwords Folios, 2002); *Blizzards of the Inner Eye* (Peterloo Poets, 2003); *The Lyrical Beast* (Salix Publications, 2004); *Skald* (Koo Press Poetry, 2009); *Pure Contradiction: Selected Poems of Rainer Maria Rilke* (Arc Publications, 2012); *Crimsoning the Eagle's Claw – Viking Poems of Rǫgnvaldr Kali Kolsson, Earl of Orkney* (Arc Publications, 2014); and *Being a Boy: early-memory poems* (e-book, Amazon, 2016). His poem sequence *Original Myths*, with etchings by Scottish artist Paul Fleming, was nominated for the Saltire Society's Scottish Book of the Year Award in 2000. *Pure Contradiction* won the Society of Author's Schlegel-Tieck Prize for translation from German in 2014, and *Crimsoning the Eagle's Claw* was a Poetry Book Society Recommended Translation in the same year.

He is currently working on a new collection of his own poetry, *Red Cave Poems*. He and his wife, the ceramic artist and print maker Wenna Crockatt, live on a small croft in North East Scotland.

Other books you may like in the
'Arc Classics' series:

Crimsoning the Eagle's Claw:
The Viking Poems of Rǫgnvaldr Kali Kolsson,
Earl of Orkney

Translated from the Old Norse
by IAN CROCKATT
with a Preface by Kevin Crossley-Holland

The Bright Rose:
Early German Verse 800-1280

Edited and translated from Old High German
and Middle High German
by PHILIP WILSON